Living in Venice

ELISABETH VEDRENNE
PHOTOGRAPHS BY ANDRE MARTIN

THAMES AND HUDSON

The author and the photographer would like to thank the
Venetians who kindly opened their doors to them and all those
who gave valuable advice. Thanks also to *Elle Décoration*.
The photographs on pages 68 and 104-105
are by Yan Martin.

Styling by Sylvie Binet
Coordination of photography by Lella de Girolami
Designed by Ideodis Création
Translated from the French by Fiona Biddulph

First published in the United States in 1990 by
Thames and Hudson Inc., 500 Fifth Avenue, New York,
New York 10110

Printed and bound in Spain by
Nuevo Servicio Gráfico Ibérico, S.A.

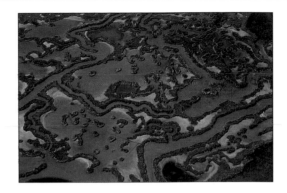

Venice and New York are cities in the guise of islands, of boats. Both provoke you: they ignite the most conflicting sentiments in you. They defy you. You can only love them or loathe them. They make you feel either crushed or thrilled. You can be lost there, terrified, but you can also discover yourself. These are "revelatory" cities. They unveil, for good or for evil, truths which are generally carefully concealed. Like photographs, they bring to light the unexposed image. Everybody has experienced this. If you leave for Venice ill at ease with yourself, you will feel excruciatingly desperate there. But if you go there full of *joie de vivre*, you will enjoy everything as you never have before and never will again.

Venice thus adds to her thousand sung beauties, which you anticipate, an unexpected magic. Never can a city have had so many transfixed lovers. As much among old stock as faithful seasonal visitors, adopted fans. And who, amongst her many idolizers, has not dreamt of one day living there? Curiously enough, those who are the most reluctant to anchor themselves in any harbour, the most solitary, are often the most obsessed by this dream.

Everything seems to have been said, written, analysed, itemized, in this incredible city. Nevertheless, the reasons for her irresistible attraction remain, happily, a mystery. It is foolish enough to want to live or, simply, to survive there. Is it precisely because it is so complicated to live in Venice, so threatening, that one wants, perversely, to taste what are said to be its final hours? To lean out once more

from a balcony and look onto an incomprehensible spectacle, with the feeling that it is perhaps for the last time. Many leave, but never light-heartedly, always out of necessity. Many others, enraptured but ignorant, arrive here: they constitute the eternal flux and reflux which have rocked Venice since she was born.

Thanks be to God there are no certainties in Venice. People who love her have faith in her. They prove it to her by continuing to perpetuate a very particular quality of life. So before discovering this art of living, let us try to understand why living there enchants people so.

Without going so far as to describe Venice as Europe's female sex, as did Apollinaire, it is clear that Venice is sexual and that she is a woman. Amongst her many feminine characteristics she has those of a mother. Humans today behave no differently from those who, fleeing the Huns a thousand years ago, sought refuge on Venice's mud banks. Attila, forever present, has changed his appearance, but the strategic swamp, the protecting foetal silt, remains around and between the crevices of the water-lily city. People of the late twentieth century continue to come and snuggle up to this maternal bosom with its colossal memory. All our past is to be found within easy reach in this womb open to the sky, in this maze of entrails, minerals and liquids.

Venice is a great house to which it is necessary to have certain keys in order to be able to gain entrance and to leave. The city is often compared to a huge mollusc; I see

it as a walnut's intricate kernel, a coiling labyrinth, centre-less, which unwinds without order, making distance impossible to judge. A box in which other boxes are boxed-in, like parts of a chimerical motor. A bottomless well. Everything here is undoubtedly disconcerting. Nothing is ever what it seems. Venice protects us and at the same time drives us wild. She beckons us and then rejects us. She captivates us, shows off to us, takes us for a ride, but gives us nothing, nothing more than impressions. She leaves us with only a glimpse, a dream. She would have us believe that she hides us, but it is she who is hiding. We think we are being sheltered but, in fact, her fortress is no more than a decoy which sends us back inexorably to our own fantasies. Venice is a sorceress, and we are drawn towards her to be bewitched.

Above all she holds us by the senses. She is perhaps the only city in our modern world to have kept a human scale. In so doing, even for Le Corbusier she is a perfect organic structure, an example to town planners. As soon as you have set foot there you rediscover sight, sound, smell, touch. Nothing less. Everything here is fluid, shift-ing, harmonious. You relearn to keep your balance. You knock against real bodies, you meet faces. In the kingdom of the pedestrian, you walk, nose in the air, eyes confront-ing other eyes, head bowed to the chevron-patterned floor, neck twisted, afraid to miss something. You become an animal once more. You start. You listen. It takes some time before you recognise the sound of your own step resound-ing on the flagstones, or detect the slapping of the water on the side of the *fondamente*, its lapping under the bridges. You hear laughter, the radio, strident feminine voices, the intertwining invectives of the gondoliers, the insufferable comments of tourists, the sliding of baskets being pulled up against the walls, the banging of a shut-ter...all the endearing little noises associated with banal, day-to-day existence, noises which no longer reach our deafened ears and which, suddenly, seem important and new, because of the way they resound against an unfamil-iar, deeply silent background.

And then there is the smell. Always strong, always acrid. Excessive. Sometimes stinking, polluted, insuf-ferable. Generally overwhelming. Disturbing, because it is so sensual. The stench of the canal and its sludge blends with occasional gusts from the high seas, and exquisite wafts of wisteria or gardenia from invisible gardens enclos-ed behind their high brick walls, slowly eaten away by win-ter fog. The walls themselves exhale smells of brine or of mosses. Strange, musky fragrances. Wet, humid per-fumes. Hotch-potch of exhalations which one is incapable of differentiating. Even the pungent saltpetre of the peel-ing walls makes you breathe in life, forgotten life.

The charm of this dead city is precisely that she is overflowing with vitality. You have to be really ill, really conformist or conventional to feel death here, where decay is so fertile. The medley of impressions, the kaleidoscope of the senses, these are what one remembers.

You live here not only to rediscover how to saunter and to stroll, but also to be a prisoner. Voluntary captivity has many attractions. You create your home like a cosy nest, a place devoted to introspection, a rampart which towers up in opposition to modern-day life.

Each interior — every one so different from the next, old or resolutely modern, minuscule, cluttered up and littered with objects or, on the contrary, spacious, practically empty, austere — each one is like an oasis, a flying carpet. Each has something obsessive about it. To live in an apparently unchanging city, a city which seems to be in possession of the secret of eternal life and to offer all ephemeral and fugitive pleasures, is to choose to live in a close relationship with the passage of time. A forgotten experience in our modern cities.

Changing and plural, an iridescent and translucent waterlily city floating in her own image, Venice can just as well appear to be a figment of the imagination. In her desire to seduce she aims to be seen as a mirror, to trick the eye, as well as the senses of smell or hearing. Not only through reflection, but also through the snare of the mask: she no longer appears caressed by light, but sketched, outlined and frozen.

She unfolds the ornate, festooned screens of her palaces, which, like curtains at the opera, entice you to go and see if the wings hold as much promise as the front of the stage. Such is the classic and perverse invitation of the mask. Venice, being a theatre for actor-spectators and spectator-actors, is the very scene of desire, of expectation and of the search for an immutable and forever-lost past. She played at being theatrical, especially during the eighteenth century, like no other city before or after her has ever done. She is still playing this role today, for outsiders and for insiders. For both are of equal importantance. The outside matches the inside, as does the exact replica of her silhouette in her aquatic reflection. All who visit Venice or who live there are conscious protagonists in this game of appearances. At times Venice looks flat, as though printed onto a surface, like the stiff stage make-up of the No Theatre, or a simple, traditional carnival *bauta*. A screen certainly, but one which serves no purpose other than to hide its true self. Venice: a double-depth drawer, a "have-you-seen-me" mask.

Outside, in the *calli* and the *campi*, you are often gripped by the strange sensation that you are inside. In a corridor or in a drawing room. And inside, everything has been made so that one has the same incongruous impression, of being outside, in the clouds, amongst the leaves. Imprisoned on its sterile stone island, this city will always harbour a nostalgic hankering for the countryside. She will always be obsessed by Nature, the sky and, of course, the sea, but also the country, its grass, its flowers, its birds, and all that is living. Forever in pursuit of this chlorophyll dream, she makes it come true at the countless parties, celebrations, carnivals and regattas, just as much as on the walls, the ceilings and the ground.

One feels a great need for a liberating dream in her frantic search for entertainment. In the eighteenth century, in Paris, there were three theatres. In Venice, there were seven. Plays were also performed privately in palaces, in the *campi* by strolling players, in puppet theatres, at the Magic Box of the New World; bull races were also run. The whole city is a stage set, everything is an act, and, should there be only one Venetian style, it would be theatrical.

This style, its decorative devices, can be found in houses throughout the centuries, constantly reinvented and then copied, reinterpreted. This is still going on today. Architects, antique dealers and decorators are having a field day, abandoning themselves with no holds barred to this sort of natural cannibalism. Venice herself secretes the reflections of her reflections and prefers distortions, exaggerations and hallucinations in space and time. You can do anything here and then to do it over again: from eighteenth-century false *barocchetto* to nineteenth-century fake neo-gothicism; from Pierre Loti's sham orientalism with travel trophies (from Kathmandu) to the counterfeit Ballet Russe style of the 1920s with Marco Polo's zestful colouring... Be inspired by the icy sophistication of Saint Mark's gold mosaics on an aquamarine background, as was the imaginative architect and interior decorator Flavio Albanese. The couturier Missoni used this idea for the floors of his apartment, reinstating the traditional profession of the *terrazziere* by creating monochrome floors (inspired by mosaics), a classic Venetian *pavement* (form of tiling). Or plagiarize (as did actress Valentina Cortese in her boudoirs decorated with frescoes) the delicious paintings under glass which are the glory of the Café Florian.

For these are the rules of the game: you must imitate everything, copy, conceal, disguise, repair, reveal, amass, repeat, make pastiches, reinvent. You must at all costs swagger, *fare spettacolo*, appear Venetian. This means everything and nothing, of course. But, curiously, everybody seeks to do it, each in his own way and according to his means. For example, you must have a little corner *à la Fortuny*. An easel, a Spanish shawl, some faded velvet draperies embossed with golden pomegranates, a large yellowing photograph, a rose, a metre of pleated silk — and that does the trick. Treat yourself, at no expense, to a fake Fortuny scent, Fortuny being the king of ersatz.

Encrust the ceilings with medallions, painted in the manner of Guardi or of Canaletto, in a sea of vanilla-coloured stucco, or mix fake marble with real antique marble from the Orient, as Piero Pinto has done with such subtlety and flair, reviving quite an ancient art. What did Pietro Lombardi do when he renovated the Gothic facade of the Ca' Dario at the end of the fifteenth century to give it a more modern, in those days a Renaissance look? He embedded rosettes of red oriental and green marble of antique origin, removed from the shafts of columns, which he applied in thin sheets. Does not Venice present itself as an immense veneer? The coral pink roughcast, the Istrian

stone tooled in the shape of diamonds, the outdoor frescoes, and the faded gilding (notably that of the Ca' D'Oro), the white serrations of fine marble...all conspire to mask the modest pink brick. All is worked for display.

The same spirit is to be found in interiors, which are decorated and dressed in every possible way. Here also the genius of cover-up rules supreme. Every morning the performance comes on again. Applications of stucco and fabric on the walls, painting on frescoes and mirrors, *terrazzo* or carpets on the floors, and furniture against the walls: naked surfaces are out. In their most diverse forms, interiors demonstrate the principles of collage, marquetry, patchwork, assemblage, fretworking, mosaic and appliqué.

There is a reason for these magic tricks. The reason goes deep. Venice owes it to herself to be light, to weigh as little as possible on her base of stakes driven into the mud, to remain flexible and elastic so as to withstand the movement of the sea (and nowadays the *motoscafi*). Hence the need for so many openings: doors at the front, round the back, on the sides, and myriads of windows to lighten the façades. Paul Morand described these houses as buildings which wish to be boats. They are shell houses — very ornate shells, definitely — but still shells. The very close relationship between the outside and the inside is therefore entirely natural.

Many contemporary Venetian architects, without playing the Venetian game to the last letter or resorting to pastiche, have nonetheless taken their inspiration from it and integrated it into their innovations. The great Carlo Scarpa restructured shops, galleries, and apartments in a modernist style often comparable to that of Frank Lloyd Wright or Le Corbusier, millions of light years away from any decoration in the Venetian style. What he retained from his city's stylistic past had more to do with working methods and traditional materials. Floors, for example, (the materials were of little importance) were laid out in the old terrazzo style. Stucco, *marmorino* and *calce rasata* were used to coat the surfaces of walls, giving them a soft,

lustrous, transparent quality. Extraordinarily inventive solutions were devised to compensate for the confined Venetian spaces: a system of partitioning walls with grills and Venetian blinds, pillars, porticoes, bridges, and spiral staircases. He used mosaic with Murano glass *tesserae*, reminiscent of Paul Klee or Klimt, for the paving at the Olivetti shop in St. Mark's Square, and also in the gold-and-black borders of the extraordinary garden which he designed in a minuscule courtyard at the Querini-Stampalia Foundation, a sort of Zen-like, oriental labyrinth, admired the world over. And finally, he revived the method (among others) of drawing *a murrine* as can be seen in the vases and dishes that he created for Venini.

The time when everything became decorative, the century when exterior decoration mixed with interior decoration, the epoch when Venice was at its most frivolous, its most ornate, but also full of life and real: Venice's greatest epoch was the eighteenth century. When historically she was at her most vulnerable, when she gave it her all, then Venice became sublime. If it is important to stop for a while to examine the Venetian style in the eighteenth century, it is because it was so harmonious and successful that it has continued to permeate every aspect of life in today's houses. It is to be found everywhere. In the eighteenth century Venice found her true style.

The preceeding century, Venice's "Grand Epoch", had been entirely devoted to the glorification of architecture. It saw the construction of imposing palaces by Baldassare Longhena (Ca' Giustinian, Ca' Pesaro and Ca' Rezzonico are amongst his most celebrated), Giuseppe Sardi, Domenico Rossi, and Alessandro Tremignon (Palazzo Labia). Venice now had the Palazzo Ducale, the Procuratie Nuove in St Mark's Square, the Convent of San Giorgio, the churches of the Salute and of San Moise.

Private residences began to imitate the palaces with their colonnades, capitals and bosses, their combination of magnificence and robustness.

At the very moment when the Republic's economy was weakening Venetians began to invest in building. The mercantile aristocracy was becoming richer and richer but dwindling in numbers, yielding ground to a class of gentlemen of leisure. The spice trade was slipping out of Venice's hands for good; ship building was declining, she was losing her colonial empire. And yet, a somewhat heavy, triumphant, baroque taste had taken over. Façades lost their pretty colours to be covered in cold Istrian stone, often carved in the Roman way. The seventeenth century also saw the birth of *palazzetti* (medium-sized houses) and of *case d'affitto* (small apartment buildings for the rental market). The middle class was assuming an increasingly important role.

So, by the turn of the eighteenth century, Venetian society was in full mutation. Venice knew that she was losing the game and, to give the impression that she didn't care, she devoted herself once more to total hedonism. No longer having the means to build (save the Palazzo Grassi

in 1748), she ruined herself on improvements. Between 1700 and 1780 the interiors of the most prestigious *palazzi* — Mocenigo, Morosini, Barbarigo, Rezzonico, Pesaro, Pisani — were done up in the fashion of the day.

Space was reorganised so as to be more intimate; smaller rooms were created within the severe Renaissance salons; there was a passion for boudoirs, concealed staircases and secret passages. Formality was forgotten. Money was thrown out of the window (figuratively and literally) to make life racy and romantic. Casings and exposed beams painted *à la Sansovino* vanished; ceilings were vaulted with plaster daub; frescoes transformed them into marvellous backdrops for the enormous Murano "pagoda" chandeliers laden with floral motifs. Crimson damask gave way to pastel moiré silks, warm and monochromatic velvets to pink and silver brocades.

Only rarely did doors retain their majestic casings of handsome red Veronese marble; the new fashion was to heighten and widen them, to decorate them with stucco pilasters and surmount them with overdoors of sculpted wood encrusted with painted medallions.

The flecked *terrazzo* floors were enriched with new colours. Attempting to imitate carpets their designs began to feature interlacing, volutes and large coloured ribbons edged with black. The celebrated Venetian tilework became a major decorative element. All work was carried out by hand by the *terrazieri* from Frioul, artisans who have passed on their craft from father to son for generations, so

preserving the tradition of binding together nuggets of real marble with lime and then beating and rolling this *granulato* layer hand-sprinkled with pieces of marble to anything from 5 to 40 mm in length. In the eighteenth century they used even larger lumps of marble.

Traditional walnut chairs and armchairs were gilded, lacquered and upholstered with precious and even more luminous silks, to match those covering the walls. Above the tables, commodes, bureaux and console tables, immense mirrors were hung, either double or in the form of pier glasses; they tended to be placed opposite windows, to reflect the light and give the rooms greater depth. It was now that the *stuccatore* had his moment of glory. He reframed, encircled, enveloped every architectural detail, emphasising it, but also, occasionally, making it disappear. For everything had to be more gentle, joyful, airy, producing a feeling of freshness rather than the suffocation induced by some *rocaille* decorations. Another particularity which has been said to characterize Venetian *barocchetto* is that it never cedes to the rococo style, considered over-elaborate and rich. The *barocchetto* on the contrary lightens, opens up and simplifies certain lines, aiming at nothing more than gracefulness and gaiety. It is in harmony with the atmosphere outside where everything rocks and sways, open parasols, flimsy gauzes, rustling fans, cascades of laughter...

Furniture became swollen, bombastic, pot-bellied in shape, akin to panier dresses or montgolfiers, and yet curiously refined at the same time. Chairs stretched out their curvaceous legs. Their arched feet raised their points into claws. Their backs became jigsaws, hollowed out to form Venetian figure-of-eight designs, indented, serrated, almost spindly. A multitude of small pieces of furniture appeared: chiffonières, tabourets, chubby bedside tables, dressing tables, tiny corner cupboards, three-footed, branched gueridons known as *giridoni*, small card tables. Round, all-enveloping and deep, the Venetian armchair was called a *pozzetto* — little well.

The walnut bomb commode held sway as did the Venetian sofa, those long banquettes seating three or four, in jigsawing walnut, elongated sister of the chair, usually placed in the enormous *portego* on the first floor, the *piano nobile*, their backs to the wall, facing each other under the great family paintings. The console, Lilliputian or gigantic, was of green or yellow lacquer, beautifully gilded like a scarab beetle, veneered all over with its often heavily laden base undulating like the tentacles of an octopus. It was on these pedestals that vases, pots and china heaters from Fontebasso or Nove were enthroned, that the *cartaglorie* of highly worked silver frames and collections of contemporary silver coffee pots were exhibited. Finally, what the Venetians called the "bureau-trumeau", first seen in the previous century, became ever taller, more arched, decorated with *rocaille* carvings in the corners... But unlike its counterpart in France, Venetian furniture featured no gilded bronze decoration.

Thus it achieved the miracle of perfect equilibrium: light, diaphanous, ornate and undulating. Sinuous contours roll up over each other whilst the purity of the overall lines is retained. The contortion remains slenderly swanlike, the undulation sketched, like nimbly played scales, their voluptuous notes resonating from floor to ceiling. Venetian furniture evokes dreams, tenderness, poetry, insouciance and fleeting pleasure: life, forever present, vibrant, ordinary, intimate.

The windows with panes like the bottoms of bottles have mostly retained their leaded panes (*a rulli piombati*) from the sixteenth century. They delighted the foreign aesthetes of the nineteenth century. In the eighteenth century, they often crowned, as it were, doors with elegant gilded or lacquered *bonegrazie*, sculpted with friezes of shells and *putti* drawing curtains. Moors or *moretti*, appeared as caryatids of ebony supporting vases or torchères, singly or in pairs, or sculpted by Brusolon on the arms and the bases of armchairs.

The three other great triumphs of this brilliant century were the use of colour, the use of mirrors and the dying embers of textile art. All sensual things made for the play of light and shade.

Ever since her foundation (contrary to the morbid myth invented by literary foreigners in search of a cultural alibi) Venice has radiated with energy and the spirit of enterprise.

Living on water without being engulfed calls for many down-to-earth qualities. The Venetian has always had his feet firmly anchored in the shifting ground and, to distract himself, kept his head in the clouds. His vitality is legendary, as is his gaiety. And this joyfulness, doubtless sometimes a little forced, achieved its apogée in the eighteenth century when the quest for quality of life became the art of living. Exhilaration manifested itself in everyday colours, in clothes, in material, but was also distilled with skill and nobility into the music of Vivaldi, Galuppi, and Benedetto Marcello; in the paintings of the Tiepolos, father and son; in the powdery pastels of Rosalba Carriera or Longhi's bourgeois, almost naïve portraits; in Canaletto and Guardi's *vedute*; in Piazzetta's playlets; in Goldoni and Gozzi's comedies; and in Casanova's stories.

A vigorous Venice, occasionally ribald, always inquisitive, never insipid. Life rings true. Sometimes it caresses, verging on the melancholy; sometimes it sparkles and banters. At great glittering feasts patrician witticisms recall the lisping, evasive responses of Goldoni's lovers, whose jokes are heard echoing around the *campi*. Everybody is aware that they must intoxicate themselves with the pleasures that still warm the heart before tasting the icy coolness of Canova's nudes...

Colours could be excessively delicate, deliberately sour. Venetians refused to use white, except in the country where they spent every summer in villas or *casoni*, and where white became synonymous with freshness. They also rejected black. They sought out all the shades which could enhance and bring to life the watery tones of the sea. They overindulged in yellow and green, greedily devoured reds, they dealt deftly with blues and golds. Frantically they sought every imaginable nuance, degree and combination, to amplify or attenuate colours under the effects of external light, to soften and reflect them in mirrors, in shimmering materials, in the brilliance of silvering or gilding. Shade was just as desirable as light. Light for the sun's rays which made the tiniest details sing, sculpting space and creating illusion; shade for the mystery of the alcove, for working a surprise effect — but certainly not for the foul-smelling reek of abandon and death that was later attributed to it.

The stucco tones were particularly soft: pistachio, aqua, eau-de-nil, absinthe, almond, lilac, pale cyclamen, peach, sugar almond pink, apricot, straw, vanilla, ochre, saffron, eggshell, buttercup, coral, azure, turquoise. Colours, often of eastern origin, climbed up vegetable mouldings and plinths, accentuating, emphasising, underlining, stressing the delicate play of plaster reliefs, or deepening the hollows of medallions on frescoed ceilings. These were the hues of artists, particularly of Tiepolo. They are the hues of the city itself, an unpredictable, unmatched palette, varying according to the hours and the seasons. And it is these unrivalled colours that people are trying to reproduce today, on walls, in fabrics.

These acidic colours, creamy but matt, correspond to the brilliant, varnished hues of lacquered furniture and brocaded silks threaded with gold and silver. For the silks, the mirrors and the glass already had a long history. In the fourteenth century, fabrics took their inspiration almost exclusively from the Far East. Byzantine figurative motifs were enriched with palms, lotus blossoms and fantastic animals. Damask arrived on the scene, as did velvet, especially Venetian *soprarizzo* velvet, worked with precious metals woven in the form of pomegranates, flowers, griffons and lions. The magnificence of these sumptuous materials — scarlet, crimson, indigo, emerald green — shines resplendently in the paintings of Carpaccio, Bellini, Crivelli and Giorgione and, later on, in those of Veronese and Titian.

The sixteenth century brought brocades woven with ornamental architectural motifs and acanthus leaves, like leaves of beaten silver, and silk velvets of beaten gold, velvets with winged animals ornamented with branches cut on a moiré background. This was the golden era: 7000 weavers were working in the City of the Doges, and their exports amounted to more than 500,000 gold ducats a year — a colossal figure! Almost every household had its loom. Raw silk arrived (after numerous detours) from the Far East and was spun and woven in Venice itself. The whole of Europe fought over these voluptuous silks, as much for clothing as for furnishing. It was then, before the rest of the world, that Venice began to dye cloth, following secret recipes. But soon "la Serenissima" would have to to cope with competition from the printed calicoes of England and France.

During the eighteenth century Venice and Florence, the Peninsula's other great textile centre, resisted valiantly, but they were unequal to the struggle. French taste insinuated itself everywhere with its leafy extravagance, its bouquets, its seedbeds of flowerets, its full-bloomed roses, its pendants, its pagodas and Chinoiseries. Venice adapted herself, although she continued to drape her impertinent darlings and her interiors in her iridescent pearly silks. On Murano, in 1763, a factory was set up to manufacture white cotton cloth from Aleppo and India,

block-printing it with fantastic, brightly-coloured oriental designs. Production of textiles remained substantial. However, the end was nigh. Nineteenth-century Venice lived on fading grandeur. The art of handcrafted textiles was gradually disappearing, to be replaced by machines and mass production.

But Venice's love of fabrics remained strong, deeply rooted in an inextinguishable passion for the materials created in her own image. The end of last century saw the revival of two factories: in 1880, Lorenzo Rubelli began to reproduce brocades, lampases, damasks, and above all intricately worked velvets (*soprarizzi*) on old looms; in 1875, Luigi Bevilacqua rediscovered old traditions and copied the colours and motifs now known as "Venetian". The prestige of these two names remains unequalled. Rubelli has expanded throughout the world, succeeding, thanks to a policy of tremendous diversification, in establishing itself everywhere. Bevilacqua, which remains smaller and more private, continues to supply the Vatican and to sell red lions on a lamé background to enraptured Japanese at exorbitant prices.

At last — conjured up in the only city where such a phenomenon could occur — began the story of Fortuny. Turn-of-the-century Venice provided the ideal setting for the flourishing of such an aesthetic temperament: in this cocoon, isolated yet cosmopolitan, Fortuny could weave silk thread without having to travel and could delve into the oriental magnificence of a past which fascinated him,

all the while free to let his nostalgic and inquisitive imagination roam. The symbiosis between man and city was so perfect that it seemed magical. Mariano Fortuny y Madrazo, a Spaniard (albeit from Granada!), was ensconced in the lagoon with his mother from an early age. Following the death of his brilliant father, a much-fêted society painter after whom he was named, Fortuny also started out as a painter. And it was above all with painter's eye that he observed Venice, gorging himself endlessly on her art, to the extent that he copied his favourite Titians and Veroneses in order to have them in his own house.

There is no doubt that he was also inspired by the carpets and by the fabrics from which the court robes and those of the ambassadors were made, the cloaks of the doges, the capes and the kaftans...by all that features in the Renaissance paintings, where rustling and rainbow-coloured clothes of Byzantium and Arabian influence shimmer, where the colours of Constantinople mingle with those of Alexandria. But it was from his mother, Cecilia de Madrazo, that he inherited his taste for sensual and tactile cloth. She used to collect antique fabrics, packing them tightly away in great chests and bringing them out to show special visitors, preferably men of letters, such as Proust or Henri de Regnier.

In 1900 Fortuny left the severe Palazzo Martinengo on the Grand Canal for the neighbouring Pesaro-Orfei, today the Palazzo Fortuny. There, aided by his muse, his French wife Henriette, he dedicated himself to recreating the

splendour of these cloths, their colours, their designs, their secrets. From talented connoisseur like any other, Fortuny became an unrivalled master. No doubt he had a highly inventive imagination. He had soon established a veritable printers' workshop, using traditional methods and creating new techniques. He took out no less that 50 patents to get rid of plagiarists — a typically Venetian attitude! His wife prepared his dyes herself, taking her secret recipes to her tomb.

One day, dazzled by the Aurige of Delphos, the fluidity of whose tunic must have reminded him of the multi-coloured and watery universe in which he lived, he created the now legendary sheath of pleated silk christened "Delphos". The half-flower, half-butterfly design of the dress (with its side-fastening of pearls and glass beads specially made at Murano) was a triumph, and he had also perfected the pleated silk whose vertical folds undulated at the slightest movement. From 1907 onwards these "Isadorables" enjoyed enormous success. First of all, of course, with dancers, from Isadora Duncan to Martha Graham, then with tragic actresses, from la Duse to Sarah Bernhardt. Fortuny's theatricality — another very Venetian quality — was reinforced by this and all of a sudden this man of eclectic passions was transformed, despite himself, into a couturier.

The dress became his calling card, launching him into a Venice which had become a refuge for international artistic celebrities, consisting mainly of English, American and French musicians, poets and writers. These were the years — between 1910 and 1920 — when the Biennale came into being, along with the Lido baths, the gondola serenades and the luxury hotels.

Fortuny completed his couture collections with dramatic designs for Greek tunics, kaftans, bournous, gauze veils, djellabahs, coats trimmed with fur, their muted or opalescent tones enriched with traditional gold and silver motifs, as well as Coptic, Indian and African motifs. Another stroke of genius in the field of textile design was his creation of a printed cotton which perfectly imitated brocaded silk, using a Japanese or Katagami stencil technique but — thanks to his ingenious, more industrial system — printing on a larger scale. This too was an instant success and Fortuny's pastel silk-like cottons soared up the walls of all the chic houses of France and America.

Then, in 1919, he opened a factory on the Giudecca which manufactured exclusively vast quantities of these gilded cottons. They were sold in his Paris shop, and Elsie McNeil was put in charge of selling them to the United States. Today it is the same Elsie, widow of Count Alvise Gozzi, who reigns over the Giudecca factory. Although now advanced in years, she is the only person who really knows how to produce those iridescent cottons that decorate the rooms of the Cipriani and Gritti hotels as well as every self-respecting Venetian drawing room.

Imagination and practical common sense were always the mark of Fortuny. These were the qualities that were admired by the Diaghilevs, the Annunzios and the Hofmannsthals, as much as by the closed, elite circle of Venetian society with whom he had forced intimate terms, a rare feat for a foreigner. Venetian high society regarded him as the city's child prodigy, an eclectic and versatile inventor capable of enlivening the masked balls (at last resurrected from their ashes) and of creating the cloth, the dresses, the lamps, the decor, the theatrical costumes and the illuminations about which the whole world talked. Everybody was talking about Venice again, at last!

Fortuny had revived "la Serenissima". The image that he fashioned was far more artificial than before and occasionally kitsch — something that Venice had never been — but increasingly successful. Fortuny succeeded where, in the same epoch, Rubelli and Bevilacqua did not, even though their copies of Venetian cloths were admirable. Even today, (although they sometimes deny it) young textile designers such as Nora Ferruzzi and Hélène Kuhn (Norelene) or Mirella Spinella continue to be inspired by his outstanding personality. And whereas today Rubelli, for example, has taken up the challenge, retaining the cachet of tradition whilst developing a sophisticated and flourishing industry, Fortuny remains a dream, a flavour, a mood, a spell.

Today, even if you have to ruin yourself a bit, allow yourself to enjoy a tiny frisson of lagunary pleasure by buying a scarlet pleated silk scarf by Fortuny at Delphos (Venetia Studium); by reupholstering an armchair in Fortuny's salmon or iced peach cotton from Trois; by rehanging your bedroom with Rubelli's fluid, impressionistic "Monet" cloth; by having curtains made of stencilled cotton with a Klimt-style mosaic design from Norelene; or by wrapping yourself in a length of precious velvet from Mirella Spinella at M Antiques... It is not so easy, however, to acquire a Delphos dress, not an original, obviously, but simply one of the limited editions which can be found at the antique dealer Saverio Mirate's or at Delphos itself.

Even more prohibitive is the famous Venetian lace!

Inventor and traveller that she was, Venice knew to observe, to make discoveries in the Orient and to bring home a host of secrets which, once adapted, were relaunched under a Venetian label to dazzle a boorish, medieval Europe. Thus lace, originally from Egypt and probably already very elaborate, miraculously reappeared with a bang in Venice right at the beginning of the fifteenth century. This is the "stitched air" that you notice so often in paintings by Carpaccio and Bellini, the much famed "rose stitch" or "Venetian stitch", as it came to be known in the seventeenth century.

Entire shiploads were exported to England whose kings were fond of it; Swiss and German merchants vied to buy it; France was so pale with jealousy that Colbert opened factories (the most famous was Alençon) just to copy it. Many Venetian lace-makers emigrated, setting up as far away as Flanders and, notably, at Valenciennes. Until the end of the eighteenth century, Europe craved lace, and in this field Venice reigned supreme.

Nowadays the situation is completely different. Lace has hardly any role in contemporary Venetian decorative art. It does not tremble like frost behind the coquettish windows as it does in northern lands. It is found only in the homes of distinguished collectors, scattered here and there on cushions, or framed like a precious relic.

This does not mean that lace-buying in Venice is no longer a tradition. Be it in Burano where, if you are not careful, there is every chance of purchasing crude imitation lace made in China, but where if you are patient, you can also go and visit the Consorzio Merletti di Burano cooperative. Here the few genuine lacemakers and embroideresses will proudly take you around their Lace Museum, where some seventy thousand original samples from bygone centuries are stored away, and where, if you are insistent enough with Maria Memo, the doyenne, you can order a small centrepiece for a table which, for scarcely thirty centimetres, will cost you some two million lira... Be it in Venice itself, at Jesurum, a distinguished house which has relaunched lace-making factories at Pellestrina and at Chioggia, and where, today, the Levi Morenos continue the traditions with a museum and a school, and offer us the last word in lace with their sheets, tablecloths and table mats which sell for absolutely astronomical sums. The same goes for the nimble-fingered Maria and Livia Mazzaron.

True Venetian lace is still that of the ogive windows with interlaced strapwork, of balconies with friezes of carved trefoils, of frothy marble crenellations crowning roofs, reflected around the interiors through the devilish play of mirrors. So once again, as it will always be, Venice appears blurred, superimposed behind its multiple veils, behind its grills and its spidery trellises, behind its openwork screens reminiscent of oriental moucharabieths.

Just as she appropriated the invention of lace, Venice the pirate also claims mirror, glass and crystal as her own. No one throughout the Renaissance could have vied with such purity, such lightness, and forms which were such a *tour de force*. A fantastic art somewhere between magic and science which was coveted and which Venice distilled with a commercial know-how based on an astute system perfect for its export network. She became the sole manufacturer of mirrors in Europe, maintaining the benefits and the secrets of her industry for a long time. A monopoly, which she defended ceaselessly against spies.

The island of Murano became a stronghold and the master glass-makers, whose kilns had been moved onto the island as early as 1291, were given immense privileges — the possibility of a knighthood amongst others — and were subjected to very severe penalties, to banishment, even to the death penalty, if they contravened the protectionist laws. Murano, a gilded prison, had to face the reality of stark competition. Colbert, who had always had his eye on the laguna, succeeded, with the help of the French ambassador, in stealing some glass-makers and installing them in the Faubourg St Antoine: they were quickly found out and, as if by accident, poisoned. Venice was keeping an eye open for trouble. Mirror-making was more than a mere fashion, and mirrors had become, on account of their beauty and their exclusiveness, a real fever.

Catherine de Medici was among the first to have a cabinet made, at the time a very fashionable object, with its "one hundred and nineteen Venetian mirrors set into panelling...". Medieval convex mirrors were to become the "sorceresses" of the nineteenth century, allowing one to see the entire room within the globe, distorted but with all its contents, so creating infinitely large spaces within an infinitely small space.

But their magic was no longer enough. People were crying out for larger mirrors, for the multiplication effect. The Hall of Mirrors at Versailles was built between 1679 and 1694. Crystals, mirrors, flames, reflections, *tableaux vivants*: all the theatrical illusory devices of the most powerful Venetian myth were in place. And the lagoon city, mirror city by essence and by definition, was adamant that it would remain the only magician able to provide this "miracle" of bedazzlement.

For her, mirror and glass are indistinguishable from her own birth. As the transparent glass is made of sand, so Venice is built on sand banks. Both are born of the same silt. Both spring forth as it were towards the beginning of the fifth century. The art of glass-making was brought to the Venetians by the Byzantines who had acquired it originally from the Phoenicians and the Egyptians. Ever since then, tight links have bound them...

Venice crystallized on this opaque water like leucoma on an eye, an eye which watches it and which makes it float on its own image. Shimmering water which reflects itself narcissistically and echoes its own light forever, a luminosity which is absorbed and immediately thrown back, diffuse and radiating. An aquatic mirror which sculpts the city. As ghostly as the silhouettes that she creates, and the spaces she transforms. This marriage

between glass and the city, and between the city and its image is still indestructible today. Inspite of crises and eclipses, and ever-present hazards.

It is a well-known fact that, one day, Venetian glass was supplanted by Bohemian glass. Venice, forever cunning beneath her ribald airs, did not hesitate to copy and work glass in the Bohemian fashion in return, sometimes going so far as to enrich this heavier, more baroque style. Venice had to survive.

The limpid Venetian *cristallino*, invented by Angelo Barovier circa 1470, and from which wine flasks, carafes, goblets and mirrors were blown with an unbridled imagination, no longer charmed either popes or kings. The great Barovier (one still refers to Barovier blue in the same sense as Veronese green) was succeeded by dynasties of glass-makers, whose exploits remain inimitable: filigree glass, streaked glass with its white spirals and grooves; frosted glass, opaque *lattimo*, a beautiful imitation of milky porcelain. Molten glass could embody every fantasy, every mannerism. It culminated in the grandiose chandeliers of the end of the seventeenth century, the celebrated *ciocca*, improved in the eighteenth century by Giuseppe Briati, comparable to a tremendous bloated pagoda, a cascade of vegetation with branches of ramshackle crystal, crumbling under polychrome flowers and decorated with candles, floating and as delicate as candied sugar.

Verve and audacity were still in evidence, but the refined elegance of former days had received a blow. Bohemia

prospered; Venice declined inexorably. By 1725, Murano had only four furnaces left. Nevertheless light still played an important role, as is illustrated by the painting *Concertino* by Longhi; *specchi a lumiera* were little mirrors, sometimes in the form of appliqué, in front of which a candle was placed, framed by the sparkle of giltwood or lacquered mirrors. Mirrors were engraved, no longer with a diamond but with a wheel, in the Bohemian way. The motifs chiselled on the surround were geometric or floral, and those in the centre depicted allegorical figures or portraits. Manufacture of *aventurine*, glittering and spangled paste, and of *lattimo*, white porcelain decorated with enamel, was also improved.

Napoleon I and then the Austrians tolled the knell of Murano's trade. In other fields as well, the beginning of the nineteenth century was a time of standstill. Whereas in Bohemia, in France and even in England, art-nouveau and then art-deco glass flourished, in Venice it stagnated.

Nevertheless in 1854 the Fratelli Toso glassworks brought about a revival of blown glass. In 1861 Abbé Zanetti established a Glass Museum (still marvellous today) and a drawing school for glass-makers. In 1866 Antonio Salviati arrived, to stimulate a new generation of master glass-makers amongst whom was Vincenzo Moretti, who succeeded in reproducing *murrine*, the mosaic motifs dating from Ancient Rome.

However, Murano remained curled up with her secrets, her unused know-how, shut up by herself in

suicidal arrogance. Until the 1920s, when an enterprising Milanese lawyer, Paolo Venini, established the Cappellin Venini Society, with a Venetian antique dealer.

Venini was going to revitalize and revolutionize the asphyxiated world of Muranese glass making. Employing the best master glass-makers on the island (Ceno Barovier, Giovanni Seguso and others), he began by reproducing classic models of the fifteenth and sixteenth century, with their wonderfully pure lines. Thus was born, designed by the painter Vittorio Zecchin, the blown glass vase known as "Veronese", a masterpiece inspired by a vase depicting the annunciation by Veronese. Its success, notably at the Art Deco Exhibition in Paris in 1925, was conclusive.

And the lesson was learnt: from now on master glass-makers, artists, architects, and designers should work together. The years 1925 to 1932 were the epoch of the sculptor Napoleone Martinuzzi, to whom is owed the creation of a new kind of glass, *pulegoso*, an opaque glass that seems spongey and granular because of its trapped air bubbles. It is often a very beautiful deep green, sometimes iridescent. The archaic forms of antique amphora vases characterize the 1930s. Then — up until the 1950s — the names of the great architect Carlo Scarpa and the Milanese Gio Ponti were to dominate the art of glass.

It is an indisputable fact that Murano was saved by the world boom in Italian design. Without it, the island would have continued to produce only marvellous reproductions, or the usual arsenal of touristic knick-knacks.

Carlo Scarpa was not only a designer. It must be emphasised that, since Venini's arrival, there had been a real collaboration between creators and technicians, sometimes creators in their turn. Scarpa, with the knowledge and the imagination of the master glass-makers, perfected *corroso* glass, with its lightly corroded surface; *sommersso* glass, its double thickness relieved by thousands of tiny air bubbles and fragments of gold; glass with reliefs; *battuto* glass, translucent and engraved, producing a scaly effect. He used threads, grooves and filigrees. Glass in the *murrine* style became fashionable once again.

As for Gio Ponti, he launched into designs that were highly-coloured, very entertaining and often anthropomorphic. The 1950s were also marked by Fulvio Bianconi's unmistakable signature. Bianconi worked a great deal with transparency, contrast and asymmetry and created what is now the classic "handkerchief" form. Nowadays these designs are highly sought after and are found only in museums and the most prestigious private collections around the world.

Once Venini had opened the way, new businesses sprang up on Murano and attracted artists and designers from all over the world. But above all they attracted Americans and Japanese — not coincidentally as they are, technically, the most advanced producers of glass. Thanks to the Memphis group and architect Ettore Sottsass's talented leadership, numerous young designers have continued to flock to the island. Sottsass, be it at Venini's, at Toso Vetri D'Arte's or elsewhere, has produced enormous quantities of vases, glasses and dishes in the most complicated wild shapes and acidic colours. Marco Zanini, Michele de Lucchi, Matteo Thun, and the Californian Peter Shire, regularly come to work with him. Provocative avant-garde objects are seen side by side with the most kitsch and the most hideous souvenirs.

Everything has become possible at Murano where glass still has infinite and, as yet, unexploited possibilities. Companies such as Salviati, Nason, Carlo Moretti, Vistosi, Eos and Barovier e Toso all have strong, avant-garde, contemporary art departments which call upon young international designers such as Heinz Oestergaard, Laura de Santillana, Gian Paolo Canova, David Paltrer, Luca Sacchetti, Hans Hollein, Izzika Gaon, Olivier Gagnère and many more. Japanese Yoichi Ohira is the designer of Majo's entire "oriental" collection, and the great Naoto Yokoyama no longer hesitates to make the journey. Today there are more than sixty glass-makers at Murano. Glass and glass-making are no longer a question of fashion, they are the future...

Pollution, incompetence, political corruption, an economy which survives by plunder on the part of shopkeepers and property speculators and egotistical investments on the part of industrial consortiums...people have even coined the phrase, "the sack of Venice". Of course she is deteriorating, asphyxiated at times by the influx of the tourist masses who poison her veins with rubbish abandoned after the carnival or a Pink Floyd concert. Of course she is depopulating. In the middle of the fifteenth century she had 100,000 inhabitants and today, less than 80,000! The haemorrhage must stop. Venice must not become a banal, fossilized knick-knack, a beggar city.

Venice is dying; Venice is languishing; Venice must be saved. We have heard these refrains for so long that they have become familiar to the point of contempt. But if living in Venice has become difficult, even a challenge, then those who apply themselves to it do so with so much love, taste and perseverance that they will defeat these apocalyptic forecasts. Venice has been on the decline for three centuries. Throughout this time we have watched over the patient, but she hangs on, ever sprightly! Of course she is no longer quite the same. Yet change (not necessarily all negative) is really the proof that if she can transform herself she will defend herself.

The 80,000 remaining citizens know that they must at all costs preserve the special characteristics of their unique city. Over the centuries they have complained, moaned, quarrelled among themselves — and been talked about. They have never resigned themselves to no longer being the independent citizens of a great Republic. It is this that will save the city. They continue to keep their heads above water, to attract the entire world into their nets. By every means, good and evil.

Meanwhile, people still dream of establishing themselves there. Venice is certainly no longer within the reach of all wallets, but the dream remains intact. Those who are lucky enough to live there — in pied-à-terre or palace — enjoy with gusto their thousand daily joys.

You have only to take an early morning walk to the Rialto market to gorge yourself on the avalanche of colours, the grey symphonies of fish, the green concerts of vegetables. Or later, seated under the plane trees of the Campo Santa Margherita, listen to the laughter of mothers pushing prams, often in a breeze which can blow away the canopies over the stalls.

On a beautiful winter day, stroll along the Zattere towards the end of the afternoon, wander among the crowds of children screeching their way out of school and the lovers eating *gianduiotto* (the traditional bar of chocolate ice-cream topped with cream), and make the most of the last rays of the sun which speckle the Giudecca canal with gold, never still, forever shimmering...

Preceding page: Aerial view of the
San Marco quarter. In the foreground
the grandiose ensemble of the Piazza
San Marco, the Basilica and the
Palazzo Ducale. Above, to the left, the
Rialto bridge spans a bend in the
Grand Canal. The Giardinetti Reali is
in the foreground.

Left: St Mark's Square, seen from the
Procuratie Vecchie, completed in
1530 by Bon and Grigi. Amongst
some of the fifty arches is the terrace
of the Caffè Quadri with its balcony
for the orchestra. It was in this
remarkable edifice that the rulers of
the Republic lived. The usual
herringbone brick paving has been
replaced by slabs of grey stone with a
geometric pattern of white marble
from Carrara.

Sestiere di San Marco
Historical centre of "la Serenissima"

Venice is a maze, and so the first thing you ask yourself when you find yourself somewhere is the name of the neighbourhood. Someone kindly responds, clarifying things for you, "near to such and such a *campo*, after such and such a canal, or in the corner of such and such *fondamenta*..." In fact, these districts known as *sestieri* are immense. Since the Middle Ages, six *sestieri* have divided the town, three on either side of the Grand Canal. On one side are Cannaregio, San Marco and Castello. On the other are Santa Croce, San Polo and Dorsoduro (to which the islands of Giudecca and San Giorgio belong). The story goes that the six teeth which are carved out of the large iron boldly crowning the prow of the gondola represent the six *sestieri*.

The San Marco *sestiere* extends from the Rialto Bridge to the Piazza San Marco, thus linking the two nerve centres of the merchant city. It sprawls as far as the Accademia bridge, in the hollow of the reversed S-bend of the Grand Canal, looking somewhat like the intricately formed kernel of a walnut. This was the district where political power was concentrated, as the Palazzo Ducale and the Basilica di San Marco bear witness, but festivities and ceremonies also took place on the enormous Piazza San Marco. In comparison, every other *campo* seems minuscule. In this cramped area the *calli* are particularly tortuous little streets, the gardens are almost non-existent, and the *palazzi*, among the most beautiful of Venice, often display no more than their backs, preferring to exhibit their façades on the waters of the Grand Canal.

Today San Marco is slightly stifling. It is not easy to get around between the classy shops, the hotels and the waves of tourists demanding glass, masks and pizzas. The most commercial streets are those of the Fezzaria and the Mercerie. Nevertheless, there are some oases: the dal Bovolo spiral staircase and the Ca' Contarini, inhabited by cats, the Fenice theatre, the Café Florian with its atmospheric painted chinoiserie rooms, the very out-dated Palazzo Fortuny... Finally, at night, or even better at dawn, Piazza San Marco. And the Basilica especially on concert evenings, shimmering with the gold of the mosaics !

Under the wonderful frieze which crowns the immense Procuratie Vecchie which once accommodated the procurators of the Republic, nestles the unique apartment overlooking the Piazza San Marco. Behind the divan are nineteenth-century Japanese rice paper panels.

From the windows in the shape of portholes, one sees the Piazzetta and the Palazzo Ducale which stands out against the San Marco basin.

Overleaf: The crowd of tourists in the Piazzetta. In the distance, the island of San Giorgio with its celebrated campanile from which one has one of the most beautiful views in Venice; the church is by Palladio. Opposite the Venetian-Byzantine architecture of the Palazzo Ducale, rises one of the two columns which bore witness to thousands of executions.

The legendary Florian café remains one of the most beautiful cafés in the world. It was opened in 1720 under the name of the Caffè Venezia Trionfante. Its little purple and gold rooms still have their 1858 decoration with cornices and paintings under glass inspired by the Orient, by Casa, Pascutti and Carlini.

Chocolate and pâtisseries on marble
gueridons are part of a ritual which
inspired Balzac to write that the
Florian is, at one and the same time,
stock exchange, theatre foyer,
reading room, club, confessional...

Contessa Lucia Zavagli Ricciardelli's apartment is pervaded by the spirit of her grandfather, the famous Venetian painter Ettore Tito, friend of Fortuny. It was his son, Mario Tito, who, after much research, rediscovered and bought back most of the paintings.

The atmosphere of the room — with its eighteenth-century walnut furniture, such as the superb bureau-trumeau, and its pale silks — is in the purest Venetian tradition.

Overleaf: On the easel, the painting entitled *La Perla*, by Ettore Tito. One recognises the delicate jigsawing chairs, typical of the eighteenth century, as well as the heavy curtains and the chandelier, indispensable components.

Walls entirely covered with paintings and drawings, consoles placed in the corners, mirrors reflecting rooms, splendid doors of veneered wood and collections of objects (here, porcelain shoes) make this apartment a typical example of traditional lagoon-city dwelling.

The yellow and green silks which cover the walls and tables are by Rubelli, the paintings by Ettore Tito. Collecting all the latest coffee pots in polychrome and gilded china was a very fashionable pastime in the eighteenth century.

A magnificent rounded and bulbous desk which reflects (another mirror game) the light filtered through the window. The latter is an imitation of old sixteenth-century Venetian windows, with leaded glass window panes.

Another corner of the office-library. Here also, signed portraits by Ettore Tito decorate the walls. In Venice, this painter was as admired as Boldini.

At the Palazzo Mocenigo everything proclaims that one is in the domain of doges. The family counted seven, of which the most famous was Alvise I Mocenigo. This is also the *palazzo* where the poet Byron lived, the talk of the town as he spent his time in the company of monkeys, parrots, dogs and a fox! Under the grandiose coffered ceiling, there is a gilded frieze with portraits of the doges in each medallion.

Right: Busts of the grandchildren of the Marquise Olga Cadaval di Robilant, daughter of the last of the Mocenigi, by Lucarda.

The salon with, to the right, a painting attributed to Tintoretto, depicting the doge who signed the peace with the Turks after the battle of Lepanto, at prayer with the pope. All the Mocenigi have one passion: music. Private concerts are still held in this salon.

The Palazzo Orfei is today occupied by the Fortuny Museum.

Above: One of Fortuny's desk lamps with an adjustable chrome lampshade and a wooden base. One model has been reproduced by Andrée Putman for Ecart International.

Left: A painting by Mariano Fortuny, set into the wall covered with different printed silks. The cushions, also recovered with silks or cotton imitating silk (another of Fortuny's inventions), accentuate the effects of superimposition and superimpression dear to the artist.

Above: The wooden staircase on rollers which Mariano Fortuny built so that he could see his works from above. Under the staircase, one of the numerous lamps, on a mobile and adjustable foot which he designed.

Left: Another of his creations, a silk lamp with arabesques, seen from below.

Overleaf: Still in the workshop, another lamp created by Fortuny, it is also adjustable and the foot can act as a container for paintbrushes and paints. On the easel is an oil representing his wife Henriette dressed in her famous Delphos dress.

Fortuny covered his walls with hangings, fabrics and pictures. He also made *trompe l'œil* frescoes and had a passion for photography. From the little window, one sees the courtyard of the *palazzo* whose façade looks onto the Campo San Beneto.

Above: The legendary Fortuny "pleats".

Left: Portrait of his wife Henriette who was his accomplice in the art of reviving printed silks. She invented new dyeing processes, secrets which she took with her to the grave.

The ancient Ridotto della Procuratessa Venier, today more simply known as the Casino Venier, is one of the rare game rooms of the eighteenth century where the decoration, in spite of the disappearance of the furniture, has remained intact.

Full of secret passages, camouflaged cupboards and spyholes, people used to play their fortune at cards, here in the midst of abundant stuccoes painted in gentle colours, worked plaster daub and mercury mirrors.

In the exquisite, chocolate-box apartment of the Contessa Antonia Foscari (another grand family of doges) one is almost overcome by vertigo. A very gay and colour-loving person, she has plastered her walls in a skilful mix of real wallpapers and false ones painted by herself. The same goes for the frames surrounding keepsake photos, most of which she has painted in *trompe l'œil*.

Above: Detail of a wall at Contessa Foscari's.

Left: A corner of the dining room with mirrors by Giovanna Giol, in a fifteenth-century palazzo on the Grand Canal. The typical jigsaw chairs of eighteenth-century Venice are painted, as are the door mouldings and the marbled frames. The burr elm table is nineteenth century, as is the whole room, imitating the eighteenth-century style to perfection!

Above: One of the many *lumières* which are a feature of the decoration of the Casetta Rossa. The intricately patterned mirrors, engraved using a wheel, were also particularly popular during the eighteenth century.

Right: A corner of the mirror-clad dining room. The walnut chairs with their curvaceous backs date from the eighteenth century. The yellow silk velvet was chosen by architect Piero Pinto. The floor is Venetian *terrazzo*, its patterns designed to look like an eighteenth-century carpet.

Above: An arrangement of flowers of fine pearls of silver and gold glass is reflected in the speckled mercury mirrors which cover the walls of the dining room. The flowers are the work of Signora Lopes y Roja, made following an old, and generally forgotten, traditional craft.

Left: The Casetta Rossa, also known as the Casine delle Rosina, seen from its garden on the Grand Canal. In the eighteenth century, the painter Guardi worked in a studio here. During the nineteenth century, writer and poet Gabriele d'Annunzio rented the house from Baron Frederick von Hohenlohe; it was here that he wrote *Nocturnes*.

The present proprietor of the Casetta Rossa asked the decorator Piero Pinto to help him to recreate a typically Venetian atmosphere on the ground floor which looks right onto the ravishing garden on the banks of the Grand Canal.

Walls hung with draped fabric the colour of eggshell, medallions encrusting the ceiling in garlands of stucco, *vedute* by Guardi and false Longhi, engraved mirrors on the doors, sofas in vanilla silk or in bronze Rubelli velvet, green material by Fortuny, boxes and low tables painted with chinoiserie... the wager is won!

On the first floor, Gabriele
d'Annunzio's room. The original
furniture — including the Directoire
bed with swans — has been
preserved while the walls have been
rejuvenated with cream silk. It was
here that the great poet was received
by Baron Frederick von Hohenlohe.

Ravishing eighteenth-century pastels look onto the desk where he wrote so many books, among them the beautiful *Nocturnes*. It was here too that his friends visited him... Fortuny, the painter Cadorin, or la Duse, the great actress of the age.

Above: Not far from Campo San Maurizio, the ancient door of a house, at the top of which is an apartment belonging to a couple of Milanese stylists, lovers of Venetian weekends.

Right: The interior design and decoration is by interior designer Flavio Albanese. As dominant colours he chose all the watery tones reminiscent of the lagoon. The painted metal staircase leads to a room under the roofs with an *altana*, a characteristic Venetian wooden terrace. The silk on the chairs is by Fortuny.

Above: Deliberately unmatching chairs and armchairs reupholstered with different Fortuny fabrics.

Left: On the green sideboard decorated with a swag of orange wood by Alberto Friso, some Murano glass the colour of water.

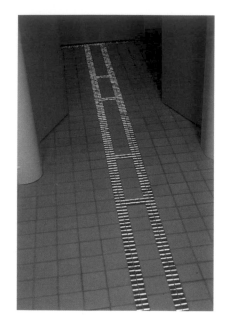

The aim of architect-designer Flavio Albanese was to explore the cool turquoise tones, warming them up with gold and playing with the brilliance of gloss paints and mosaics. Taking inspiration from Byzantium and the Basilica San Marco, he amused himself by running gold lines, like Ariadne's thread, along the floor, the skirting boards and the doors. Flavio Albanese also designed the chimney.

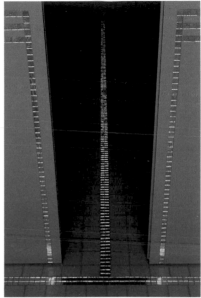

Simply reupholstered in white silk, a pompous-looking gilded armchair recalls, with a wink, the network of gold which criss-crosses the entire house. While the doors (often sliding) and the cupboards are turquoise, the walls are pale grey with a satin finish. The floor tiles are of *pâte de verre*.

Above: Made entirely of gold mosaic, the Oriental thread, so dear to Klimt, even straddles the tables.

Left: The framework of this table recalls the design of the window guard rails. All the tables are by Flavio Albanese.

Above: In the glass cupboards a collection of very fine, transparent, gold-tipped Murano glass.

Left: A very sophisticated and subtle game of gold and turquoise geometry makes the narrow corridor seem immense.

Over the perfectly square interior courtyard is an example of the inventiveness of Antonio Foscari and Gae Aulenti, who were responsible for restoring and restructuring the Palazzo Grassi. Purchased not long ago by Fiat, this eighteenth-century *palazzo*, built by Giorgio Massari for the Grassi's of Bologna, represents the swansong of Venetian civic architecture. Today it is one of the most visited *palazzi*, thanks to the prestigious exhibitions which are held here.

Above: A staircase, rethought and repainted in peach by Gae Aulenti.

Right: Three flights of grand staircase lead through the loggia to the first floor, towards the luminous space of the courtyard. All around are sumptuous *trompe l'oeil* paintings, a reminder of the parties and pleasures of a dizzy century.

Above: An impressive sixteenth century chimney with cariatides in the Ca' Contarini delle Figure which is on "la volta del canal", the elbow of the Grand Canal.

Right: The theatre director and set designer Pier Luigi Pizzi who lives here has accentuated the classical allure of this palace. Inspired by the decorative style of Antiquity, he positioned two fake marble obelisks in the hall of the *portego*. The *terrazzo* floor is superb, and prompted French poet Theophile Gautier to write eloquently on the subject in *Italia* (1852).

Two busts are silhouetted against the windows of the Ca' Contarini delle Figure. Commenced by Giorgio Spavento and completed by "Scarpignino" at the beginning of the sixteenth century, this *palazzo* gained the description "delle Figure" on account of the cariatides supporting the balcony of the *portego*. The façade is also decorated with heraldic trophies.

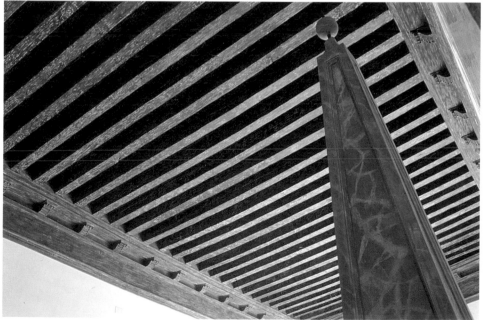

Left: The splendid ceiling with exposed beams painted *à la Sansavino*.

Details of the magnificent Renaissance chimney of the Ca' Contarini. All in marble and stucco, a fine bust of Romain bursts forth from a shell edged with gold over a frieze featuring columns and skulls of cattle. The chimney has pagan and Triglyph overtones.

Above: The extraordinary chimney under the medallions which run all around the room, under the ceiling.

Right: A corner of the dining room in a magnificent coral-salmon colour. The plinths that edge the terrazzo floor are painted in almond green; the painted column supports a Moorish bust. Before Pizzi lived here, the palace belonged to Jacopo Contarini, mathematician and botanist, and intimate friend of Palladio. Wagner was a visitor here.

Previous page: Symphonies of gilding at the Fenice theatre. Sculptures in wood and gilded stucco and medallions decorate one of Italy's most beautiful theatres. Burnt down in 1836, it was faithfully rebuilt, retaining its eighteenth-century appearance. The interior decoration is by Nino Barbantini. Operas by Rossini and Verdi were first performed here, and Visconti portrayed its atmosphere beautifully in the film *Senso*.

Looking onto the Grand Canal, the library of this *palazzo* boasts one of the most sophisticated stuccowork ceilings in Venice. Henry James, a frequent visitor, was lucky enough to sleep here and never forgot it! The pale ochre and pearl tones are reflected in the engraved mirrors of the tall secretaires. Monet had a studio here and the jazzman Cole Porter held memorable parties here in the 1920s.

Above: A beautiful stair-cupboard, designed by Scarpa, with Japanese touches and refined geometric details: veneers of two different woods and partitions coated with *calce rasata* the colour of fresh butter.

Right: A beautiful door made of pear and other warm woods.

Above: All the office furniture was designed by Scarpa and produced in pearwood. The ceiling is coated with black stucco. Here the partitions are of wood and the windows are in the form of loopholes.

Left: The entrance to the office. Exposed beams, black ceiling lights, sliding doors, opaque glass screens, steps: everything is carefully thought out to maximise space.

Above: A *baccaro* (home of Bacchus) where Venetians love to meet before lunch or dinner to drink something roughly equivalent to an apperitif: that is a glass of white wine known as *ombra*, or a fruity red wine, such as the strawberry scented *fragolino*... And to eat: the inevitable yellow cubes of *polenta* (semolina), *nervetti*, strips of beef), minced veal livers, sardines in *saur*, and a thousand other very special snacks. Most of the *bacari* are found on either side of the Rialto bridge.

Right: The painted blind of a grocer's shop window.

Left: Carpaccio at the most famous bar (and restaurant) in Venice, Harry's Bar. Like the Bellini cocktail made with peach juice and the Tiziano, made with grape juice, Carpaccio was the invention of Arrigo Cipriani (above), one of the proprietors. Harry's Bar became famous in Paul Morand's day, and was relaunched by Hemingway and Orson Welles. It is still the meeting place for writers and duchesses, politicians and influential Venetians, as well as international celebrities. The risotto served here is exquisite and the service is personal and faultless.

Above: In autumn there are a great variety of marrows and pumpkins from which the excellent soups and succulent risotti of Venice are made.

Left: Fresh pasta: coloured ribbons of different-sized tagliatelle.

Above: Beside the Grand Canal and under the wonderful arches of the Fabbriche Nuove designed by Sansovino, the fishmarket teems with activity and noise every morning. Crabs, molluscs, seafood, eels and small fish such as sardines are brought from the lagoon.

Left: Tender artichokes, to be steamed with a sprig of mint.

The interior courtyard of the fifteenth-century Palazzo Centani where Carlo Goldoni was born in 1707 and where, today, the seat of the Institute of Theatrical Studies is situated. The traditional outside staircase behind the well is a rare survivor with its roof and gothic arcades so typical of Venetian *palazzi*. The floor is also antique — *a spina*, that is made of bricks arranged at angles to form a herringbone pattern. In days gone by, all the *calli* of Venice were paved in this way.

Sestiere di San Polo

The Rialto: heart of the city

Just as the San Marco *sestiere* weds the lower curve of the Grand Canal, so the San Polo quarter nestles in its upper loop. The two are connected by the Rialto bridge, until the nineteenth century the only bridge on this royal way. Just as at San Marco one breathes in the air of ceremony, the aura of gracious manners, secrets and affairs of State, so at San Polo one is intoxicated by the bustling and colourful activity of the merchants. Because it was around the Rialto — Venice's vital lung, a kind of Wall Street of its age — that all business and commerce was done.

This vast ensemble of Renaissance buildings spreads out from the foot of the bridge around the Campo San Giacomo and along the Grand Canal, where, as soon as the first gleams of morning appear the boats of the market gardeners still make their way from the mainland, weighed down with fruit and vegetables and accompanied by loud cries. The San Polo district has remained unpretentious, and while it prides itself on having some very beautiful *palazzi* (in particlular the Ca' Pisani-Moretta and the Ca' Albrizzi) it has retained its popular and traditional way of life, and numerous artisans still live and work here. The vast and rustic-looking Campo San Giacomo dell 'Orio and the Campo Santa Margherita with their little old men seated under the plane trees, their dolls' house architecture, and their morning markets, remain, thankfully, beyond the path of the average touristic circuit.

In San Polo one can still come across charming spots, old bridges which span criss-crossing canals, little one- or two-storey *palazzi* with washing hanging from their windows behind neglected little gardens from which emerge cypresses, *altane* covered with wisteria, and oleander. There are taverns, *bacari* where one can sample *ombra de Tocai* and eat snails, and there are animated, family *trattorie*. At the centre of the district rises the enormous Chiesa de Santa Maria Gloriosa dei Frari, nicknamed the Ca' Grande. Its severe brick façade masks the most flamboyant *fiorito* gothic façade in Venice. Only a couple of steps from here is the Scuoladi San Rocco, its walls and ceilings plastered with Tintoretto's masterpieces. Finally, another unusual and often deserted spot is the area around the magnificent Scuola dei Carmini with its façade by Longhena and the Chiesa dei Carmini with its huge and peculiar cloister and garden.

Above: A detail of the fifteenth-century façade of the Ca' Pisani-Moretta on the Grand Canal. Famous throughout the town for its ceilings painted by Tiepolo, it is one for the few *palazzi* still belonging to its original family, the Pisani, of whom Count Sammartini is the descendant. He has preserved with patience and passion the grandiose spirit sought by his ancestor Pietro Vettore Pisani, curator of St Mark's.

Right: The glow of candles is reflected in the old silvering of a mercury mirror.

The great ballroom on the *piano nobile*. The eighteenth-century ceiling is painted with frescoes by Giovanni Guarana. The blown glass chandeliers from Murano throw light from real candles. Terrazzo floor, stucco piers and eighteenth-century consoles complete the picture.

Overleaf: Still in the *portego*, the great central salon on the first floor, the immense doors of polished walnut open onto the interior courtyard, reflected in the floor as though in the waters of a canal. The fine openwork chairs are typical of eighteenth-century Venetian *barocchetto*.

Detail of *passementerie* over the
curtains of the "yellow room", a sort
of gallery of ancestors where
numerous portraits hang on walls
draped with yellow silk. Over the
gilding is a frescoed ceiling depicting
Virtue and Destiny, painted by Angeli
in the seventeenth century.

Right: More eighteenth-century baroque decor, reflected and deformed in a wall of antique mirrors. Everything moves, everything is duplicated, just like the two cupids (above) in one of the many paintings adorning the various rooms of the *palazzo*. The gilded wall brackets, the mirrors and the painted child's pram are also typical of the eighteenth century.

In a *palazzo* on the Grand Canal,
another example of the Venetian
passion for collections. Here, a
collection of silverware and beautiful
apothecary's jars in painted and
engraved Murano glass.

Above: In another room, detail of a chiaroscuro painted ceiling in the nineteenth-century style.

Right: A collection of splendid silver church vessels.

The Grimani family library in the Ca' Civran Grimani. This classical palace of Palladian inspiration and built of Istrian stone is on the corner of the Rio della Frescada and the Grand Canal. The Grimani family, which can count three doges among its ancestors, is passionate about history and music. The stuccoes are eighteenth century.

Right: A typical Venetian "arrangement": candlesticks and silverware on the marble top of an eighteenth-century console against a wall decorated with stuccoes painted in delicate colours. Floral garlands create a fresh effect while wall brackets and candles are reflected in the *specchi a lumiera*.

Above: At the home of Princess Esmeralda Ruspoli many portraits of the princess, such as this one, adorn the walls.

Right: A magnificent *pulegoso* glass 1930s vase from Venini's. Designed by the sculptor Martinuzzi, it was discovered by antique dealer Roberto Pedrina.

A corner of the bedroom. As is so
often the case in Venice, the ceiling is
low. The walls are hung with
drawings and paintings depicting
theatrical scenes or the mistress of
the house. Artists include Lila Nobili,
Ettore Tito, Clerici and Leonor Fini.

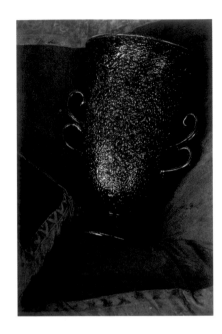

Above: A *pulegoso* vase by Napoleone Martinuzzi.

Right: Details of a couple of the works by Fabrizio Clerici.

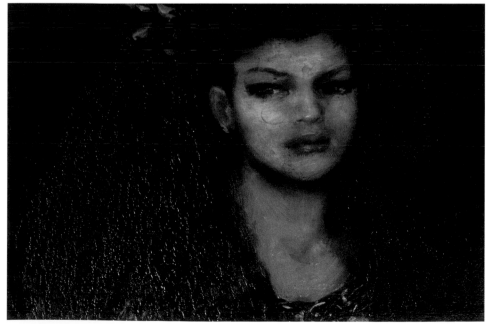

Above: A very light room with windows looking out over the Chiesa dei Frari. Brightly-patterned Oriental and Indian carpets are evocative of Venice's past.

Left: A magnificent portrait of the Princess Esmeralda, painted by Lila de Nobili.

Overleaf: The cloisters of Santissima Trinità, the most imposing of the two cloisters of the monastery of the Santa Maria Gloriosa dei Frari. A terrace with a beautiful balustrade runs all the way around. In the centre there is a huge well with columns crowned by statues by Cabianca. Within the heart of the crowds, this a magical, deserted place.

The facade of the Ca' Zane, once the Casino Zane-Habsburg (1695-1697), on the way to the Rio Marin. Although now in state of disrepair, it still has the beautiful iron grills on the ground floor, the traditional balustraded balcony with three windows in the centre opening onto the *portego*, the central hall on the first floor, and pretty sculpted heads on the outside. Architects: Antonio Gaspari and Domenico Rossi, two big names!

Left: A portrait of Otto von Habsburg who bought back the Ca' Zane — in those days called the Casino Polcenigo — with its music room and its *ridotto*, the old games room. Today nothing remains but the finely worked and enchanting shell.

Overleaf: The marvellous casino with an astonishing wooden balustrade (sculpted by the renowned Brusolon) and a ceiling (created around 1700 by Stazio) with stuccoes and *putti* almost as beautiful as those at the Palazzo Albrizzi. The frescoes depicting *putti* astride lions in immense shells are by Nicolo Bambini.

Details of cherubs and *putti* supporting medallions among branches, painted in fresco or sculpted in stucco. These stuccoes are among the great Abbandio Stazio's first works.

The casino's delightful little garden.
Casini or *ridotti* were traditionally
well hidden at the bottom of a secret
garden.

Above: In the eighteenth century, the ground floor of the house where Emmy Puppa lives was occupied by a *frittolin*, a seller of fried fish, a typically Venetian figure that has now disappeared.

Right: Through the peach-coloured curtains, one makes out the bridge which gracefully spans the Rio dei Caffaro. The appartment, at water level, is in a fourteenth-century house sometimes called the Ca' Rossa.

The proprietor of the Ca' Rossa is a great collector of ancient lace and rare linen cloth. Here also, superimposition and accumulation, characteristics of the Venetian art of living, are in evidence.

Above: This little house is on a corner between two canals. Columns, exposed beams, polished floor, gilded mirrors, small pieces of furniture and a profusion of fabrics create the charm of the interior.

Left: The peach and salmon silk matches this splendid lace bedjacket, the collection's chief treasure.

Piles of cushions of a infinite variety of laces: a symphony of whites. All the openwork and embroidered stitches remind us that Venice was the first great lace centre.

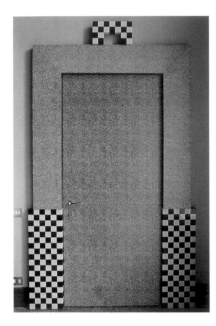

Above and right: Three examples of door frames typical of Ettore Sottsass's style in the Memphis Group period. Sottsass conceived the entire appartment with his accomplice and friend, goldsmith Cleto Munani. In the salon the traditional *terrazzo* floor complements Sottsass's vermicelli decor. In the foreground is a sofa by Michele de Lucchi.

Above the immense grey-mauve sofa (designed, like the rest of the furniture, by Sottsass) is a painting by M. de Suvero. During the 1980s, Sottsass was an initiator, a guide, and an inspiration for all the designers of the Memphis group that was the symbol of new design throughout the world.

Above: A Murano glass dish by Carlo Scarpa. The famous architect created something new when he adopted the ancient *a murrine* (mosaics) technique.

Right: Under the old beamed ceiling, four halogen lamps with light diffuser discs in glass crown the piece of furniture on the opposite page.

Above: Detail of one of the four columns supporting the four lamps. Although fantastic, these totem-poles are crammed with practical details.

Left: The huge multiple-use piece of furniture (bookshelf, desk, bar, cupboard) which Sottsass designed specially for Munari in 1984. The desk is black lacquer. On the left side, another lamp, perpendicular to the ground, lights a gueridon, also part of this piece of furniture.

The dining room designed entirely by Sottsass: on the black lacquer table, two silver-plated metal fruit bowls by Scarpa; in the distance on the console, candlesticks by Alessandro Mendini; to the right, another piece of furniture with multiple uses, in the shape of steps and made of cypress wood (Sottsass, 1984).

Blue dish, really a sculpture in glass,
made on Murano by Izzika Gaon,
curator at the Museum of Jerusalem,
in "homage to Cleto Munari"; the
latter has produced a complete
collection of glass at Murano.

Above: The ceiling with *trompe l'oeil* frescoes gallantly overhangs the avant-garde dining room!

Right: Flanked by two black lacquer chairs, the sideboard by Sottsass plays with different marbles.

Above: An "unbalanced" jug in silver-plated metal, by Angelo Mangiarotti.

Right: A silver-plated metal dish designed by the great Austrian architect Hans Hollein.

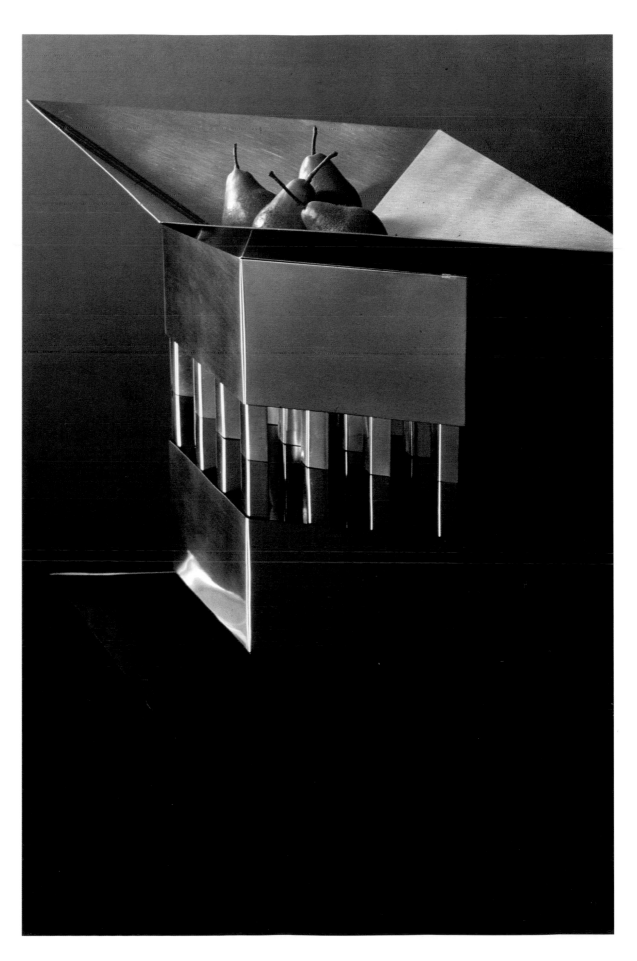

View of the Rio degli Ognissanti (parish of San Trovaso). At the end of the *fondamenta* and behind the bridge, is the cupola of the Chiesa degli Jesuiti (1726-1736) by Giorgio Massari, the façade of which looks onto the Zattere. The interior frescoes on its vault are by Tiepolo. The small low building houses the last little shipyard or *squero*, where gondolas are still made and repaired.

Sestiere di Dorsoduro

Oasis of tranquillity and secret gardens

On its long, back bone-like ridge, wedged between the Grand Canal and the large Giudecca Canal which leads to the port, the Dorsoduro district has, little by little, become one of the town's most fashionable. This is because of its large number of gardens, which are small, but very secret and very well-kept, bordering the ravishing *fondamente*; because of the Chiesa della Salute with the Punta della Dogana at its prow, giving it the appearance of a ship; because of the Fondamenta della Zattere, that immense quay where you are sprayed by sea foam and where you can spend all afternoon warming yourself in the sun while watching the incessant passage of all sorts of boats: ranging from great international liners to ferries, agitating the water as they pass and making waves lap at your feet as if it were the sea.

Once it was the preserve of artists (Vedova and Music still live here); Peggy Guggenheim cottoned onto this when she chose to live here. Today every square metre has been listed, raked, replanted or restored. Up to and including the last intact *squero* in front of San Trovaso. All made of wood, coquettish and flowery, it is under constant fire from photographers because it is the sole survivor of the forty odd little naval workshops that, until the beginning of the century, were dotted around Venice. Gondolas are still made and repaired here.

Some people have chosen to live in cloisters, others (like Piero Pinto) in a redundant chapel or (like painter Roberto Ferruzzi) in an ancient boat house. A pleasant and calm atmosphere reigns, an atmosphere peculiar to the residential parts of all towns. Even if, little by little, the grocers and the bistrots are ceding their ground to art galleries and glass show-rooms, and if, at times, authentic Venetian life is giving way to the purely picturesque, Dorsoduro remains a delightful quarter where everybody knows everybody and where the feeling of being sheltered, removed from the crowds is jealously preserved. The extensive Zattere has remained very animated and is invaded by the Venetians for the traditional Sunday walk. The Accademia Museum continues to attract people from all over the world. On the way to the Maritime Port are two landmarks that must not be missed: the Chiesa di San Niccolo, isolated in a deserted and almost surrealist spot, and the house known as "the monkey man's", inhabited by a character straight out of a painting by Carpaccio.

Above: The corner of the dining room at the home of painter Roberto Ferruzzi, better known as Bobo. He settled into this house-studio in an old boathouse fifteen years ago. One can feel the passion for objects which has guided this family of antique dealers for generations. On the whitewashed wall there is a very beautiful collection of plates from all over the world and a *veduta* painted by Ferruzzi himself. The dark walnut chairs are late sixteenth century and come from Tuscany and Lombardy.

Right: A successful combination of precious and unusual objects.

Above: A remarkable chair against a background of logs.

Left: A magnificent twelfth-century Byzantine Virgin and Child in painted wood. She has jointed arms and can thus be used for processions. In the background is stencilled fabric by Hélène and Nora, Ferruzzi's wife and daughter, who produce such magnificent materials under the label Norelene.

Above: A head of sculpted wood for a study of the Passion — here tears — in the style of Luca Della Robbia.

Right: Silk painting by Norelene, bringing to mind Byzantium and Klimt — and the reflections of the lagoon. The Ferruzzi have always been great lovers of cloth: Roberto's father, friend of Mariano Fortuny, collected it.

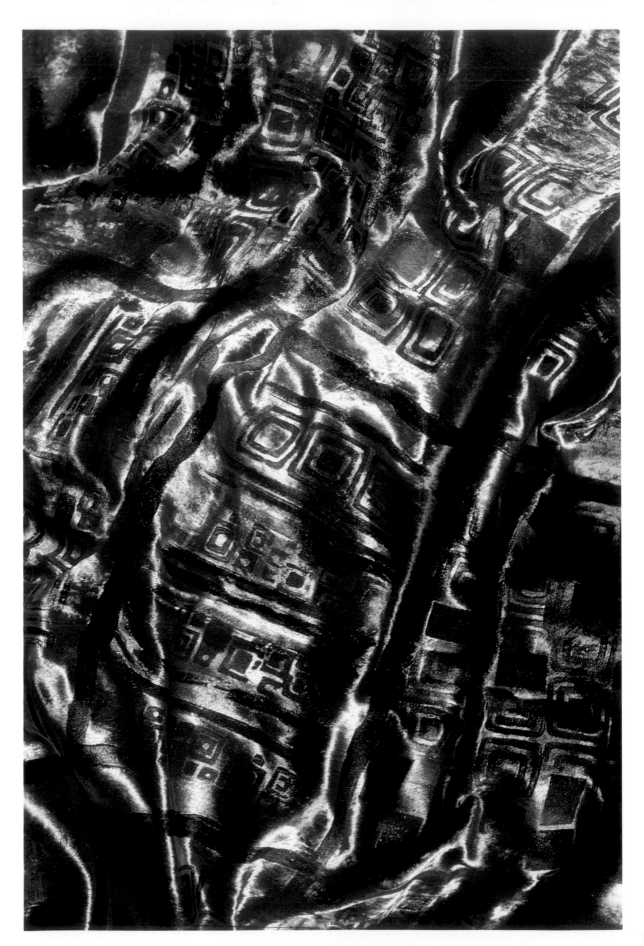

A corner of the sitting room. All the fabrics, as well as the hat and the shoes, are by Norelene. The paintings are by the master of the house. To the right is the very rare Byzantine Virgin and Child.

Above: A cotton fabric hand painted by Nora and Hélène Ferruzzi in the colours so beloved by Venice: blue and gold.

Right: The immense wooden stencils which the two women design and make themselves.

Norelene's two good fairies in the middle of their work. Their compositions of juxtaposed geometry and abstraction are real paintings. Like everybody in Venice, the city which seems to have invented the secret, they jealously guard their dying methods.

Overleaf: Lying on their sides like silvered fishes, bellies in the air, gondolas await the expert hands of the carpenters of the *squero* of San Trovaso to be sanded down and repainted, and the hands of the *tagliatore* to carve the oars and the *forcole*, their support. The gondola is the very symbol of Venice.

Detail of the facade of the Ca' Dario, punctuated by circles, often in sevens like lotus blossoms, and set with coloured marbles like precious stones. Built by Lombardo during the Renaissance for Count Giovanni Dario (who was often in Istanbul negotiating peace with Mahomet II or in Persia), the Ca' Dario has a sophisticated Oriental air and echoes the little church of Santa Maria dei Miracoli, also inlaid with coloured marbles and from the same period (c 1487).

Above: A close up of *rulli piombati* windows, like bottle bottoms surrounded by lead.

Left: The secret staircase with Renaissance marbling on the walls.

Overleaf: Behind the splendid commode, said to be by Condé, and beneath the Murano pagoda chandelier with branches of blown, coloured glass, an immense Brussels tapestry (Franz Geubel's workshop, 1535) depicts a battle between Scipio the African and Hannibal.

Above: Detail of a grotesque mask from the nineteenth-century panelling which covers the dining room walls.

Left: Reflections in glasses engraved with floral motifs, created by Salviati.

The dining room, redecorated in turn-of-the-century taste, looks onto the Grand Canal. The chairs, with their figure-of-eight design, are characteristic of the Venetian eighteenth century. Today this sumptuous palace is inhabited by the daughter of the great industrialist Raul Gardini and her husband, son of Arrigo Cipriani, a couple of young VIPs.

In the entrance hall of the architect Riccardo Gaggia's apartment, beautiful engravings decorate the walls. On the ground floor, the walls are covered with planks painted with white gloss. This is a common practice for protection against damp. Note the low ceiling (another common feature) and, on the floor, the beautiful polychrome marble marquetry designed by Riccardo Gaggia. A masculine apartment with a whiff of Englishness.

Above: A corner of the salon. On the ground floor of a rather dilapidated *palazzo*, Riccardo Gaggia has succeeded in creating a two-floor apartment as comfortable and intimate as it is small.

Left: On the walls of the interior staircase, as indeed throughout the house, the master's passion for obelisks is demonstrated. Another Venetian collector!

Above: Not far from the Ca' Venier dei Leoni, now the Guggenheim Museum, and right next to the Ca' Barbarigo (easily recognised by its mosaic-covered façade), the Ca' da Mula is a very beautiful gothic *palazzo*. The legendary blazing-haired Contessa Morosini lived here at the turn of the century. This *palazzo* was also immortalised by Monet. Pictured here, the garden façade.

Right: On the *piano nobile*, the grand floor of this fifteenth-century *palazzo*, a marvellous eighteenth-century composition of stuccoes and frescoes in *grisaille* and *trompe l'oeil* depicts the muses. In the foreground, the miniature armchair with its unusually large "paws" could be a toboggan.

Under the magnificent fifteenth-century Sansovino-style ceiling with painted beams, a very pure ten-branch Murano chandelier in blown and twisted glass. The walls are covered with an ancient red damask printed with gold.

The beauty of this room in the Ca' da
Mula is that the filtered light catches
the different greys and old gold paint.
As usual, there are mirrors
everywhere, veneering the walls or
inlaid into the panelling. Like the
stuccoes and the *marmorino* on the
piano nobile, the painted garlands are
eighteenth century.

Another symphony of pearl grey and gold in the little chapel. In former days all the *palazzi* had their own chapel. This is one of the rare ones still in existence, meticulously preserved above all by the Alesi, the present occupants.

For Loredana Balboni's house, Carlo Scarpa succeeded as usual in enlarging spaces by dividing them up, and at the same time, making openings and playing with grills and netting, creating the effect of an Oriental moucharaby.

Above: Grills designed by Scarpa replace the traditional windows *a rulli piombati*. The garden is reflected inside the house on the top of a glass table. The general effect is owed to Oriental — even Japanese — inspiration.

Left: Another example of the Venetian passion for collecting.

At Loredana Balboni's, an Iranian
ceramic plate on a background of
marmorino (or *calce rasata*), that
mixture of marble powder and chalk
traditionally used in Venice. Scarpa
used it a good deal, appreciating its
pale tones and its gentle and lustrous
effect.

A marble torso and Persian vases:
very ancient objects, rare and pure
forms which realise their full
significance in Scarpa's austere and
sometimes museum-like spaces.

Generous curves characterise the banister and the staircase designed by the great Venetian architect Carlo Scarpa for the house belonging to Loredana Balboni. Scarpa worked on the conversion for ten years (1962-1972). The steps are of marble and the walls are covered in the highly polished, ivory-like *marmorino* (a traditional plaster on a base of powdered marble and chalk).

Above: At the mouth of the huge spiral staircase, perfectly poised on its marble pedestal, is a geometric sculpture of yellow, pink and black metal, designed by Francesco Zanon. The long and narrow windows are typical of Scarpa.

Left: A piece of pottery from Iran, part of the vast collection of Persian vases that is especially treasured by the mistress of the house.

147

Above: Two particularly fine carnival masks made entirely of minuscule glass beads from Murano. Today, only the Baroness Nella Lopez y Rojo carries on this craft. She also makes ravishing flowers, in shimmering tones.

Right: The enigmatic smile of a late eighteenth-century beauty.

Above: Another unusual object, an anthropomorphic china vase. The Venetians, travellers in reality and in spirit, also travel in their imagination and are crazy about any curious or remarkable object.

Left: A very rare *trompe l'oeil*-painted "commode-trumeau", well-rounded and bulbous as they so loved them in the eighteenth century. It imitates the window of a cabinet of curiosities containing shells and corals. The chairs covered with absinthe-green silk have the characteristic back of the Venetian *barocchetto*.

Above: On a rush-bottomed chair made by a countrywoman, one of the first Eve terracotta sculptures by Silva Berndt. The floor is in *terrazzo*. Alma Berndt had the floor of the neighbouring Ca' Rezzonico copied by a *terrazziere*.

Left: The first floor at Alma and Silva Berndt's, entirely furnished in the Biedermeier style. Above the beams, paintings and drawings by friends have been amassed.

Above: In front of a sumptuous green Fortuny silk hanging, souvenirs of musical evenings on the carved wood Liberty sofa, purchased in the south of Italy. A bronze head by Silva Berndt on an unusual stool from the Ca' Dario.

Left: The whole house, at once sophisticated and bohemian, lives to the rhythm of art.

Above: Venice and the Orient: a turn-of-the-nineteenth century wood and *papier mâché* Buddha from Thailand, reflected in a mirror with a late seventeenth-century gilded frame decorated with dragons and little cherubs.

Left: Hung in a room of yellow, gold and green tones, paintings by Sebastiano Ricci and Longhi and pastels by Rosalba Carriera.

Like every self-respecting Venetian, Ucci Ferruzzi is both a great antique dealer and a great traveller. His house reflects his own image, full of the charm of someone with an innate understanding of the art of composition.

Ettore Tito, famous Venetian
painter and friend of Fortuny
and the poet Gabriele d'Annunzio,
bought a small gothic *palazzo* on the
fondamenta which borders the Rio
di San Barnaba. He restored it in
about 1905 and established his
workshop there. Today, his son,
Luigi Tito, also a painter and sculptor,
lives in this magical palace entirely
decorated by his father.

Above: Like a Flemish still life,
a corner of the room with a basin.

Right: All the elements
of a Venetian dining room
are brought together: the little
Moroccan table set with mother of
pearl, a sculpture by Jiuseppe Tito,
jigsawing chairs with the famous
figure-of-eight shaped back,
stuccoes on the walls and on the
ceiling, flames from the wall
brackets and candelabra reflected
in a Liberty mirror.

Above: The marvellous washed-out stuccoes of the ceiling which Ettore Tito found in a *palazzo*.

Left: Detail of a corner of the immense workshop where Luigi Tito still works.

The other end of Luigi Tito's long dining room. The parquet is a reproduction of the *a spina* brickwork of the Venetian *calli*. The marble columns are from Africa and the frescoes were taken from the wall of a small house on the banks of the Brenta, between Venice and Padua. They probably date from the seventeenth century. On the table, a sculpture by Luigi and, on the easel, a canvas by his father Ettore. The old-fashioned, worn-out curtains add charm to this strange place, the genuine domain of artists with sophisticated taste.

Left: A delicious still life lit by the traditional Venetian window with its *rulli piombati* panes. These windows even feature in paintings by Carpaccio.

Right: Another poetic corner. In the foreground, a sculpture by Luigi Tito and an arrangement of faded hortensias stand out against the blurred background of curtains and frescoes. Everything here has a soul, contributing to life but never dominating it.

Above: The little church on the
Campo San Vio, rebuilt in 1860. This
is where architect and interior
designer Piero Pinto chose to take
up residence.

Right: The walls have been pointed
and the brick and marble left bare.
Under the lion, symbol of Venice, a
sofa is covered with a magnificent
fabric imitating marble.

The salon is in the nave of the
church. Pinto plays with the effect of
different colours of marble, some
there originally, others added. The
metal staircase leads to a mezzanine
suspended in the air, a sort of
gangway leading to small rooms like
alcoves. An abundance of precious
fabrics, marble busts, spheres and
carpets create an atmosphere where
Orientalism and Classicism meet.

Overleaf: Piero Pinto has gathered a
beautiful collection of those Venetian
paperweights that were once mass-
produced and that the author Colette
so adored. Made with *murrine*, little
segments of glass sticks which
resemble flowers following ancient
Roman tradition, these *mille fiori*
balls enjoyed a revival during the
Romantic period.

Pinto shows himself worthy of
Venetian taste in his collection of
glasses, dishes, flagons and pots of
glistening and glowing colours from
Bohemia, Venice and Turkey. The
Orient is present in every detail, the
master of the house having been
born in Egypt.

Above: An unusual little English armchair in mahogany.

Right: A small collection of various ivory and mother of pearl boxes, from different places and different epochs, shines in the small darkened room scarcely lit by the four-lobed gothic oculus, like a church window.

The fairy-tale marble lace façade of the Ca' d'Oro in the Cannaregio sestiere. Nicolo Contarini built this palace at the beginning of the fifteenth century. Its portico recalls Byzantine palaces with the added fantasy of flamboyant gothic. It was called the "house of gold" on account of the gilding and frescoes that once covered it. Only recently opened to the public, one can now see its masterpieces by Titian, Bellini, Tintoretto, Tiepolo, Carpaccio and Giorgione.

Other Sestieri

Cannaregio, Castello and the Giudecca

The Cannaregio district is little known to tourists who cross it rapidly on the Strada Nuova on their way back to the station. However, although poorer and more remote, it has much to offer for those who take the time to explore: the Campo SS Apostoli so dear to Canaletto; the area around the Chiesa di Gesuiti; the astonishing Ghetto Nuovo, immortalised by Visconti in *Senso*; the narrow Cannaregio canal, once the main thoroughfare for traffic to the mainland; the Rio di Noale, another important canal which issues into the lagoon after passing the marvellous Misericord Abbey. In fact, the whole of Cannaregio looks to the north of the lagoon, hemmed in by the Fondamenta Nuove, which is as large as the Zattere, but colder and more austere. From here people embark for the islands and, at dawn, the *caoline* and the *sampierotti* leave to go fishing.

Castello is more cheerful and varied. Planned around the Arsenal which was its stronghold and *raison d'être*, it is not so long since it echoed with spirited shouts emanating from numerous small factories, boat houses and *squeri*. On one's way to the Giardini, on the crossings of the Via Garibaldi, one is sometimes lucky enough to meet bead threaders and embroideresses sitting at their front doors. There are four particular treasures: the Chiesa di San Giovanni e Paolo, proudly guarded by the statue of Colleone; the Qucrini-Stampalia library; the delightful Chiesa Santa Maria dei Miracoli; and San Giorgio dei Greci, the home of Carpaccio's most famous paintings. Finally, Castello boasts the most beautiful promenade along the Saint Mark basin: the sunny Riva dei Schiavoni from which one gets a sumptuous view of Venice.

The Giudecca consists of eight islands following each other nose to tail. It is here that the biggest kitchen gardens and gardens are tucked away. On one side one can admire the whole city spread out like a fan, from the other the whole of the lagoon. Nowadays the artists who set up on this last bastion of tranquillity have stars or businessmen for neighbours, no doubt because life here is more spicy than elsewhere. At either end of the Giudecca is a particular point of interest: the enormous and dilapidated Mulino Stucky, whose silhouette stands out impressively against the setting sun, and the highly celebrated Cipriani Hotel, the most luxurious in Venice.

The incredible *trompe l'oeil* frescoes covering the walls and ceilings of the Palazzo Labia are reflected in a beautiful mercury mirror. Even though it does not look onto the Grand Canal, this baroque *palazzo* is one of Venice's most majestic, known above all for its frescoes, some of which are by Tiepolo — a rare thing!

On the Cannaregio Canal, the Palazzo Labia was built circa 1750 by the architect Tremignon for the Labia family who, so it is said, were so rich that they used to throw their gold dishes out of the windows. Its previous owner, Carlos Besteigui, gave memorable parties under the frescoes of the palazzo: the last of these, a costume ball held in 1951, is still legendary.

Overleaf: The great salon and the Tiepolo frescoes at the Palazzo Labia. This is what Maurice Rheims, Chief Auctioneer, said in 1964, at the time of the sale of the "last palazzo to disgorge its riches": "only the Tiepolos will remain; bound to their lot on the wall of the empty house: the negro with the strawberry, the white horse, the gallery of musicians, the embarkment of Antony and .

Cleopatra, the greyhound with the centurion, the perspective of the silver dishes..."

Above: The workshop where Mirella Spinella produces her splendid silks, hand-printed in the old way. The silks are stored in painted cupboards.

Right: The Barchessa, the boathouse adjoining the Palazzo Lezze (built by the great Longhena), today the residence of Mirella Spinella. This charming house is at water level.

A corner of the library. The brick walls have been left bare and the floor is tiled with terracotta. Apart from fabrics, the mistress of the house has two other passions: travel and the animal sculptures which she brings back. The nineteenth-century Venetian transparent glass and iron chandelier is quite rare.

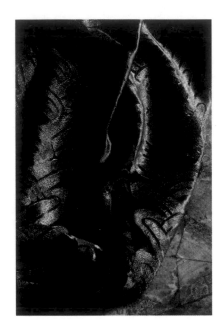

Above: Detail of a purple velvet printed with gold antique patterns. Textiles by Mirella Spinella are sought after by all the great Italian decorators.

Right: Around the sixteenth-century chimney, a sophisticated bric-à-brac of precious objects. In the background, one can make out a rhinoceros from India.

Above: Another view of the same room, full of nooks. Tapestry, Liberty glass, plants and Japanese drawings evoke travel across time and space in the Marco Polo tradition. On the table is another rhinoceros, in jade, from China.

Left: A superb pile of old-fashioned, delicately-tinted Fortuny cushions.

Above: Detail of a piece of lace with architectural designs recalling the lacy marble of the city, executed by the nimble-fingered Mario and Lina Mazzaron.

Right: An old photograph of a lace-maker against a tablecloth and napkins edged with fine Jesurum lace.

Above: In his workshop at the Laboratorio Barvarie delle Tole in the Castello quarter, an artisan moulds a *papier mâché* (*cartapesta*) frame.

Left: Detail of highly skilled embroidery by Maria and Lina Mazzaron.

Above: Colours and weights in front a window looking onto a charming garden at Orsoni's mosaic workshop.

Right: Detail of a gold angel from the mosaics of the Basilica San Marco. The Orsoni brothers were commissioned to restore all the mosaics of the Basilica, particularly those in gold.

The Orsoni workshop where great squares of *pâte de verre* are stored and cut, ready to become mosaic *tesserae*. The *tesserae* are cut by women working with strange instruments like outdated sewing machines.

Left: A worker at the Orsoni workshop in the process of withdrawing *pâte de verre* from the oven.

The ground floor of the Pinacoteca Querini-Stampalia has been completely redesigned by Carlo Scarpa, even including the little bridge which spans the Rio di Santa Maria Formosa. Here the architect gave free reign to his taste for marble and for the play of cubes fitting one inside the other, geometric forms, split levels, staircases, suspended bridges and grills.

At the entrance to the Querini-Stampalia Foundation with its feet in the water of the canal, Scarpa retained the ancient arch and the. bare brick, and set lines and squares of gold into the white marble.

On the *piano nobile*, an orgy of stuccoes in delicate and creamy colours, dating from the seventeenth century, with marble busts by Canara de Marinali. The Ca' Querini-Stampalia dates from the beginning of the sixteenth century. Today it is library of repute.

The painted and stuccoed decoration at the Foundation is particularly beautiful and well-preserved. The floor is of *terrazzo a pastelloni*. The celestial globe is by Gilles Robert de Vaugondy (Paris, 1688-1760) geographer to the King. In the little rooms decorated with staff garlands there is a series of beautiful Longhis portraying Venetian life and its eighteenth-century parties as well as scenes by Bella.

Details of geometric designs in the garden at the Foundation, redesigned by Carlo Scarpa. The works were carried out by the Venetian architect between 1961 and 1963. These are pure forms, verging on the metaphysical or the Zen, and combining different materials and colours: marbles and concrete, whites and greys.

An ancient well within a maze of different geometric blocks, channels fountains and paths through the lawn. This ground construction with very elaborate details considerably enlarged the small, narrow, rectangular garden: an example of modern Venetian *trompe l'oeil*.

Above: Transparent ashtrays from Murano on a low glass table. Through the table one can see the geometric pavement designed by the Missonis and carried out according to the most traditional and ancient techniques. Comfort and simplicity reign here as in all Missoni houses.

Right: Designed by the Missonis — who are fashion stylists — the originality of this house lies in its use of *terrazzo* to create a contemporary style floor.

Above: Pale sofas, cushion fabrics by Missoni, and in the foreground, the squares and colours of the floor, reminiscent of a Missoni carpet!

Left: A low-ceilinged room made into duplex, as is so often the case in Venice. Everything is done to enlarge spaces which are always too small. The walls are of ivory *calce rasata*.

Above: The facade of palazzo "dei Tre Oci" (the three eyes) looking onto the Fondamenta delle Zitelle, on the banks of the Guidecca Canal. It was built for the painter Mario De Maria, known as the "painter of moons", at the turn of the century. Its three enormous ogive windows are like three great eyes, looking onto the most beautiful spectacle imaginable: the San Marco basin and, in the distance, the Palazzo Ducale.

Right: A very beautiful but austere piece of sixteenth-century furniture; in the distance the full-length portrait of a solemn man, entitled *The Philosopher*, is by Adolfo De Maria, son of Mario and also a painter.

Behind the jointed wooden mannekin, often used as a model by Adolfo De Maria, a portrait of his wife Adele, by the painter himself.

Most of the sombre and massive furniture in this strangely charming place, is, like the house, in a mock early Renaissance style dating from the turn of the century.

Above: A corner of the dining room.

Left: A small room, like an alcove, with Nile-green curtains. The painting, entitled *The Man who Writes*, is signed in Latin (Marius Pictor). It is a portrait by Mario De Maria of his father-in-law, Robert Voigt. This oil was exhibited at the 1909 Biennale.

Above: Valentina Cortese's bedroom is a veritable pastiche on the Florian café. It was the actress herself who conceived the interior decoration of her appartment on the island of Giudecca, looking over the water to St Mark's — with the help of her friend, the legendary architect Renzo Montgiardino.

Right: A detail of the decoration: a portrait of Valentina in the Oriental style.

A corner of the bedroom: reflected in the mirrors and in the glass covering the watercolours, the many candles create an illusion of space. The painting and *trompe-l'oeil* effects are the work of Fabio Palmidese, a pupil of the great scenographer Lila de Nobili.

Another romantic view of Valentina
Cortese's appartment with paintings
by Fabio Palamidese.

The salon with *trompe l'oeil* frescoes, arbours, real and fake sculptures and wonderful real and artificial flower arrangements. In this jewel of an appartment decorated by an actress, it is natural that the art of illusion should be the art of life.

The painter Geoffrey Humphries also fell in love with the Giudecca. Based in Venice for 24 years, he established himself, before anyone else, in a superb loft-workshop in an old factory.

Above: The wonderful light from the windows looking onto the Giudecca emphasises the simple, uncoordinated furniture often purchased for practically nothing at second-hand dealers on the island.

Right: Some Thonet chairs and a flamboyant opera screen for this music lover.

Above: Long buffalo horns on the piano, ready to reverberate at the next party.

Left: A typical example of the modern taste for Orientalism so dear to the inhabitants of Venice, where heterogeneous bohemian decoration has been raised to the rank of a device. Beside paintings by the artist, old Venetian or Oriental fabrics are suspended as though in paintings by Carpaccio or Bellini...

The immense kitchen at the Casa Frollo on the Giudecca. Marble table, *terrazzo* floor, Thonet chairs and spick-and-span kitchen utensils create a very warm atmosphere. There was once talk of the possible sale of this legendary *pension* to Americans or Japanese. The place was so popular that one had to reserve a room six months in advance. But finally, it came to nothing and the Casa Frollo will soon be reopened, completely restored, as charming as it ever was.

Above: The extraordinary copper utensils, with pumpkins and autumn bouquets.

Overleaf: In the summer the lagoon resembles a vast, downy prairie of reeds and grasses. The sugary scent of tamarisk mingles with the tang of salt. Islands of wild, overgrown vegetation conceal the *valli*, the name used by Venetians to describe pools reserved for fishing and shooting wildfowl.

One of the stages in the production of a long, red-veined vase in Venini's workshop. The glass must be worked very swiftly, with the aid of tongs, while it is still hot and malleable.

Above: An enormous vase, swollen in form, dating from the 1920s. From a private collection.

Right: Still in Venini's workshop, the master glassmaker, having removed the molten ball of glass from the furnace, blows it and turns it into a mould.

Above: Sculptor and glassmaker
Vistosi is in the very first stages of
cold-sculpting an enormous block of
glass.

Left: Three wavy-stemmed corolla
glasses designed by the great Cleto
Murani and made for him on
Murano. Munari, who has produced
objects for numerous designers,
notably those of the Memphis group
in the glorious years, is now
designing and producing his own
collection.

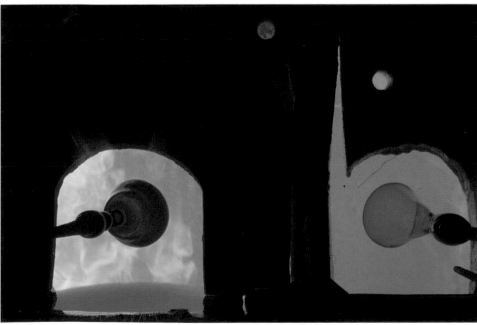

A ball of molten glass at the end of a long pipe is blown by the master glassmaker. He has to be remarkably speedy and precise, like a dancer at the ballet, withdrawing the molten glass from the fire, blowing it with force, and turning it with deft skill.

Above: Little bottles in the shape of spinning tops created by the Japanese Yoichi Ohira for De Majo.

Right: Today the island of glass also produces the most avant-garde creations designed by the greatest international creators. Murano has been relaunched in terms of economy and of fame.

Above: Carafe and glasses by Marcello Furlan, produced at Murano by L.I.P. (Snc).

Left: A three-legged cup full of humour, created by the master glass-maker Lino Tagliapietra for the Californian architect Peter Shire who worked for a while with the Memphis group. Next to it, a tall totem-like vase by Ettore Sottsass.

Overleaf: The Torcello campanile stands out against an immense sky behind a sea of poppies, a garden typical of the island, with climbing vines, cypresses and umbrella pines. Although very rustic, Torcello is one of the lagoon's best-kept islands.

On the island of Burano little fishermen's cottages and the leaning campanile are reflected in a canal, creating a pool of colour. Burano brims with brightness in the middle of the glaucous, silver lagoon, comparable to an advertisement for pots of paint.

Above: The *casupole* of Burano fall into line like toy houses. Because of the sea air they are meticulously repainted every year, always in naïve colours, each house different from the next.

Left: The inhabitants have made decorative details a matter of honour, as testified by this unusual dormer window surround.

Above: The interior of a *cason*, a kind of rustic hunting and fishing lodge, still found in the southern *valle* of the lagoon towards the Po delta. People gather around the *foger* (hearth) to smoke game and heat the enormous cooking pot. There are stuffed herons at the windows and engravings of ducks on the traditional panelled walls.

Right: Trucks pick up the latest catch of fish.

A *cason* with its characteristic long outside chimney. Austere, originally always thatched, the *casoni* are massive edifices, hidden in the secret twists and turns of the *barene*, the banks of sand and mud. They used to be the Venetians' favourite holiday homes.

Overleaf: Cormorants, herons, sandpipers, ducks and all the marshbirds, with their caps and their waders, evoke the untamed, Robinson Crusoe-like life of the lagoon. Longhi's paintings often feature long guns like the one on the wall, designed to enable one to shoot when sitting in a boat.

Home from fishing and shooting. The boats are kept in wooden sheds, often piled up to lean against the *cason*. The nets are also kept here, as are the *studie* (reed mats laid out on the bottom of the boats) and various wooden decoys.

Stuffed birds are exhibited in a simple painted wooden cupboard. The lagoon is rich in wild duck and in all species of waterfowl - as well as mosquitoes and rabbits!

These are typical views of fishing on a *valle*, a kind of pond where eels, sardines, mullet and sea bream are caught in *lavorieri*, reservoirs encircled by nets.

All the fish are sent to the market in Venice, where they can be eaten on the spot, cooked on huge grills. In the spring you can also find the famous *moleche*, those little crabs caught at the time when they are changing their shells.

Overleaf: An aerial view of the lagoon depicts its mysterious and ever-changing patterns of channels and *barene*.

Venice

FABRICS

Silk

Norelene

Campo S. Maurizio, San Marco 2606, tel: 5237605.

Hélène Kuhn and Nora Ferruzzi's silks and velvets are printed with designs reminiscent of Byzantium or Klimt.

Antichità e Oggetti d'arte

Frezzaria 1690, tel: 5235666.

Mirella Spinella's sumptuous silks and velvets reflect the purest Venetian spirit. Interior decorators fight for them.

Luigi Bevilacqua

Santa Croce 1320, tel: 721384.

The most precious, the most costly brocades and damasks, handmade as in days of old.

Rubelli

Campo San Gallo, San Marco 1089, tel: 5236110.

Mouthwatering Venetian-style silks and cottons for interior decoration.

Trois

Campo San Maurizio, S. Marco 2666, tel: 5222905.

As well as authentic antique silks, Ketty Trois has exclusive rights to Fortuny cottons.

Lace and Embroidery

Musco del Merletto-Consorzio merletti di Burano-Scuola di merletti

Piazza Galuppi 183, tel: 730034, à Burano.

Veritable temple of Burano lace and embroidery, some of which dates back three hundred years. Maria Memo, founder of the cooperative, teaches young girls the different lace stitches, including the "Burano" stitch.

Jesurum

Ponte della Canonica, San Marco 4310, tel: 5206177.

Overflowing with table cloths, sheets and curtains, embroidered or in "Venetian point".

Maria Mazzaron

San Provolo, Fondamenta Osmarin, Castello 4970, tel: 5221302.

Here nimble fingers can make you anything you wish to commission.

BOOKBINDERS

Piazzesi

Santa Maria del Giglio,
San Marco 2511, tel: 5221202.

*Specialist in "carta a bagno", paper made in vats.
These boxes and packaging are the most famous
in Italy.*

Paolo Olbi

Fondamenta Nuove,
Calle del Fumo 5310, tel: 5285025.

*Another specialist in "carta a bagno". Makes very
beautiful booklets and diaries, and rebinds old
books.*

Alberto Valese

Salizada San Samuele 3135,
tel: 5200921.

*Specialist in "carta marmorizzata", paper made
to imitate marble following ancient Oriental
techniques.*

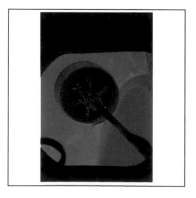

MASTER GILDERS (LACCATORI, DORATORI)

Barutti Alfredo

San Marco 4231, Campo Manin,
tel: 5287316.

Cicogna Michele

Campo San Tomà, San Polo 2867.

Zanin Stefano

Picina di San Samuele,
San Marco 3337, tel: 5285346.

Cavalier Gianni

Campo San Stefano, San Marco 2863,
tel: 5238621.

MASKS

Laboratorio Artigiano Maschere (Giorgio Clanetti)

Barbaria delle Tole (près de S.
Giovanni e Paolo), Castello 6657,
tel: 5223110.

*The oldest mask-maker, and also the most faithful
to tradition.*

*And don't forget the flowers and masks beaded
with antique glass: Contact: Baronne Nella Lopez
y Rojo, Dorsoduro 866, tel: 5234829. The
Baronne is one of the very last who knows how to
work this very ancient craft, a craft which has
almost completely disappeared.*

GLASS

On Murano

Barovier e Toso

Fondamenta Vetrai 28, tel: 738049.

Carlo Moretti

Fondamenta Manin 3/13, tel: 739217.

Toso Vetri d'arte

Fondamenta Manin 1, tel: 739955.

De Majo

Fondamenta Novagero 29,
tel: 739988.

Seguso Vetri d'arte

Ponte Vivarini 138, tel: 736655.

Società Veneziana Conterie

Fondamenta Giustiniani 1,
tel: 739922.

Glass beads only.

Museo Arte Vetrario

Palazzo Giustinian, Fondamenta
Giustiniani 8, tel: 739586.

In Venice

Venini

Piazzetta dei Leoncini,
San Marco 314, tel: 5224045.

*The most innovative since the 1950s. Famous
names include: Gio Ponti, Carlo Scarpa,
Wirkkala, Marco Zanini, Ettore Sottsass, etc.
Glassware; also chandeliers and standard lamps.*

Salviati

San Gregorio 195, tel: 739286.

*Classic glass. Many reproductions. Very
sophisticated.*

Pauly

Castello 4391, tel: 709899.

*A gigantic showroom - breathtaking. Chandeliers
to dream about...*

L'Isola

Campo San Moisé, San Marco 1468,
tel: 5231973.

*This shop has recent work by all the great
designers.*

Orsoni

Cannareggio 1045, tel: 717255.

*This workshop was responsible for the restoration
of the mosaics of St Marks.*

ANTIQUES

Pietro Scarpa Antichità

Via XXII Marzo, San Marco 2089,
tel: 5227199.

*Magnificent drawings, some from the
Renaissance, others by Tiepolo... About to open
another shop: Galleria Antichi, Campo San
Moisé, Tel : 5222697.*

Francesco Mirate

Calle Della Verona, San Marco 1904,
tel: 5227600.

Pippo Casellati

San Marco 2404, tel: 5230966.

High period style.

Barozzi

San Marco 2052, tel: 5289615.

Seventeenth century Venetian.

Beppe Patitucci

Campiello della Feltrina,
San Marco 2511, tel: 5236393.

P. Emmanuele Zancope

Campo San Maurizio,
San Marco 2675, tel: 5234567.

For lovers of extremely old glass.

Roberto Pedrina

Two shops : l'Ixa at Campo Santo
Stefano, tel: 5229656, and at the
Piscina San Samuele, tel: 5221580.

*Expert in Venetian glass, from the late eighteenth
century to the 1960s.*

Ninfea

Calle Lunga Santa Maria Formosa 5228.

Antique clothes, fabrics and lace.

ART GALLERIES

Il Cavallino

San Marco 1725, tel: 5210488.

Il Naviglio

San Marco 1652, tel: 5227634.

Il Capricorno

San Marco 1994, tel: 5206920.

These are the three most famous art galleries in Venice.

Galleria Barnabo

Calle Manipuero, San Marco 3073, tel: 5200673.

The most recent and the most avant-garde.

Galleria Venice Design

San Marco 3146, tel: 5207915.

Exhibits notably the works of Cleto Munari and Ettore Sottsass.

Not to be missed : Peggy Guggenheim museum, exhibitions at the Palazzo Grassi and the famous Biennale (Cà Giustinian, tel: 5200311).

BOOKSHOPS

Each of the shops listed below has a particularly well-stocked section on Venice.

Libreria Sansovino

San Marco 84, tel: 5222623.

Libreria Internazionale San Giorgio

Calle Larga XXII Marzo, Ponte San Moisé, tel: 5238451.

Libreria San Giovanni e Paolo

Castello 6358, tel: 5229659.

Libreria Editrice Filippi

San Lio, Calle del Paradiso, Castello 5762, tel: 5235635.

Works published by father and son, often in Venetian. An institution.

FLORISTS

Flowers are rare and very expensive in Venice. You can buy them at the Rialto market early in the morning or at the following shops:

Fantin

Campo San Salvador, San Marco 4805, tel: 5226808.

Biancat

Campo San Polo 1474, tel: 5206522.

Fioreria San Marco

tel: 5228583.

CAFES AND PATISSERIES

Caffè Florian

Piazza San Marco

Living up to legend, the most mythical place. Chocolate and "Corto Maltese" cocktail.

Caffè Quadri

Piazza San Marco

Charming old-fashioned decor.

Pâtisserie Marchini

Calle del Spezier, Santo Stefano 2769.

Pâtisserie Rosa Salva

Campo San Luca.

BISTROTS : I BACCARI

Very popular, the place to have a ritual "ombra", a pre-supper drink (glass of white wine) and to eat the traditional "cicchetti": "baccala mantecato" (cod) with a cube of polenta, or the saltier, very Venetian "sarde (sardines) in saor". One often ends up by dining here. Simple and traditional cooking.

Do Mori

Calle do Mori.

Antico Dolo

San Polo 778.

Specialities are tripe and offal.

Il Volto

Calle Cavalli, San Luca 4081.

Reputed for its wines.

Osteria del Milion

Corte del Milion, San Giovanni
Crisostomo 5841.

*And lastly : Do Spade (Rialto 860), Alla Vedova,
Ca D'oro (Calle del Pistor, Strada Nova,
Cannareggio 3912).*

RESTAURANTS

Corte Sconta

Calle del Pestrin, Castello 3886,
tel: 5227024.

*Founded by Hugo Pratt. Still a meeting place for
artists. Specialities are fish and seafood, always
very fresh.*

Poste Vicie

Pescheria Rialto, San Polo 1608.

*Grilled fish and famous "tagliatelle in camicia
nera".*

Caffé Orientale

San Polo 2426, tel: 719804.

Very good "risotto alle seppie".

Da Ivo

Ramo dei Fuseri, San Marco 1809, tel:
5285004.

Al Paradiso perduto

Rio della Misericordia,
Cannareggio 2540, tel: 720581.

Stays open very late.

Do Forni

Calle degli Specchieri,
San Marco 457, tel: 5232148.

*Famous vegetable risotto. The interior is a replica
of the restaurant car of the Orient-Express.*

Da Franz

Fondamenta San Iseppo,
Castello 754, tel: 5220861.

*Refined. Much frequented during the Biennale -
see visitor's book.*

Alla Madonna

Rialto 594.

*Its genuinely Venetian atmosphere makes up for
the mediocre food.*

Locanda Montin

Dorsoduro 1147, tel: 5227151.

Romantic in good weather.

Harry's Bar

Calle Vallaresso, San Marco 1323, tel:
5285331.

*Hemingway drank here. You can sip the house
Bellini or eat the "Carpaccio" or "risotto agli
scampi" for which this restaurant has become
famed around the world.*

Harry's Dolci

Sant'Eufemia, Giudecca 773,
tel: 5224844.

*One of the most beautiful views in Venice, and the
celebrated name of Cipriani.*

L'Altanella

Rio Ponte Lungo 268, Giudecca,
tel: 5227780.

*Under a pergola, one of the most delicous places
in Venice.*

Locanda Cipriani

Torcello, tel: 730150.

A must.

Da Romano

Via Galluppi, Burano.

*Whatever the season, it is always advisable to
book a table.*

La Fura Tola

Cale Longa San Barnaba,
Dorsoduro 2870, tel: 5208594.

Dona Onesta

Dorsoduro 3922, tel: 5229586.

Paris

LINENS

Missoni

43, rue du Bac, 75007 Paris,
tel: 45 48 38 02.

Dolce Notte

208, bd St-Germain, 75006 Paris,
tel: 45 49 40 20.

Frette

48, rue du Fg St-Honoré, 75008 Paris,
tel: 42 66 47 70.

Christian Benais

18, rue Cortambert, 75016 Paris,
tel: 45 03 15 55.

GILDER

Jean Alot

101, rue de Patay, 75013 Paris,
tel: 45 82 80 32.

GLASS

Quartz

10, rue des Quatre-Vents, 75005 Paris,
tel: 43 54 03 00.

Diva

97, rue du Bac, 75007 Paris,
tel: 45 48 95 39.

CHANDELIERS AND MIRRORS

Veronese

184 bis, bd Haussman, 75008 Paris,
tel: 45 62 67 67.

Todeschini

13, rue St-Florentin, 75008 Paris,
tel: 42 60 12 74.

Au vieux Pierrot

24, rue de Maubeuge, 75009 Paris,
tel: 48 78 06 06.

MIRROR RESTORATION

Perrier-Rolin

85, av. Ledru-Rollin, 75012 Paris,
tel: 43 43 13 12.

LIGHTING

Artemide

62, rue J-J Rousseau, 75001 Paris,
tel: 42 33 06 17.

CERAMICS

Marazzi

17, av. de la Grande-Armée,
75016 Paris, tel: 47 64 10 53.
Carreaux émaillés traditionnels.

Farnese

47, rue de Berri, 75008 Paris,
tel: 45 63 22 05.

Carreaux anciens et rééditions.

FOODSTUFFS

Raggi

49 bis, av. Franklin-Roosevelt,
75008 Paris, tel: 43 59 10 93.

Finadri

47, av. de la Motte-Picquet,
75015 Paris, tel: 47 34 54 09.

Ghezzi

51, rue Descamps, 75016 Paris,
tel: 45 04 99 92.

Au Village Italien

50, bd du Temple, 75011 Paris,
tel: 47 00 81 52.

RESTAURANTS

Bellini

28, rue Le Sueur, 75016 Paris,
tel: 45 00 54 20.

Sormani

48, rue du Gal Lanzerac, 75017 Paris,
tel: 43 80 13 91.

La main à la pâte

35, rue St-Honoré, 75001 Paris,
tel: 45 08 85 73.

Villa Vinci

23, rue Paul Valéry, 75016 Paris,
tel: 45 01 68 18.

London

RESTAURANTS

Villa Medici

35 Belgrave Road
London SW1
tel: 071-828 3613

Venice Restaurant

65 Great Titchfield Street
London W1
tel: 071-636 5618

Cecconi's

5a Burlington Gardens
London W1
tel: 071-434 1509

Ziani Dolce

112 Cheyne Walk
London SW10
tel: 071-352 7534

Laguna Restaurant

50 St. Martins Lane
London SW1
tel: 071-730 6327

L'incontro

87 Pimlico Road
London SW1
tel: 071-730 6327

Vecchia Riccione

11 Upper St Martins Lane
London WC2
tel: 071-836 5121

Santini

29 Ebury Street
London SW1
tel: 071-730 4094

Signor Zilli

41 Dean Street
London W1
tel: 071-734 3924

LINENS

Frette

98 New Bond Street, London W1Y
tel: 071-629 5517

Lunn Antiques

86 New Kings Road, London SW6
tel: 071-736 4638

Artemide

17 Neal Street, London WC2
tel: 071-240 2346

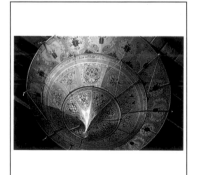

MIRRORS

Through the Looking Glass

563 Kings Road, London SW6
tel: 071-736 7799

GENERAL

Harrods

Knightsbridge
London SW1
tel: 071-730 1234

Liberty

Regent Street
London W1
tel: 071-734 1234

FOODSTUFFS

Camisa, I & Son

31 Old Compton Street
London W1
tel: 071-437 7610

Lina Stores

18 Brewer Street
London W1
tel: 071-437 6482

La Picena

5 Walton Street
London SW3
tel: 071-584 6573

GLASS

Murano Studio

103 Marylebone High Street
London W1
tel: 071-487 4436

Venetian Glass Gallery

44 Fulham High Street
London SW6
tel: 071-736 9131

Venice - Murano Glass

63 Grange Avenue
London N12
tel: 081-446 3879

U.S.A.

FABRICS, ANTIQUES

Portantina Ltd.

886 Madison Avenue
New York, NY 10021
tel: 212-472-0636

LACE

Felsen Fabrics

264 West 40th Street
New York, NY 10018
tel: 212-398-9010.

S. Beckenstein

130 Orchard Street
New York, NY 10002
tel: 212-475-4653

Weller Fabrics

54 West 57th Street
New York, NY 10019
tel: 212-247-3790

GLASS

Caprice

9301 Tampa Avenue
Northridge, CA 91324
tel: 818-886-8788

C & A Fine Importers

919 Calle Amanecer
San Clemente, CA 92672
tel: 714-361-9556

Crystal Palace Imports

809 West Harbor Drive
San Diego, CA 92101
tel: 619-232-6096

Geppetto Import & Restoration

31143 Via Collinas
Westlake Village, CA 91362
tel: 818-889-0901

Dasynal Corporation

8832 West Pico Boulevard
Los Angeles, CA 90035
tel: 213-276-1111

Italian Accents

7751 York Street
Welby, CO 80229
tel: 303-288-4781

J & J Design Inc.

1321 Sunkist Place
Anaheim, CA 92806
tel: 714-533-3111

Park Avenue

790 Market Street
San Francisco, CA 94108
tel: 415-788-7203

Aventura

463 Madison Avenue
New York, NY 10024
tel: 212-769-2510

I. Magnin

3050 Wilshire Boulevard
Los Angeles, CA 90010
tel: 213-382-6161

Muriel Kavasak Ltd

1094 Madison Avenue
New York, NY 10028
tel: 212-535-7851

Neiman Marcus

1618 Main Street
Dallas, TX 75201
tel: 214-741-6911

Tiffany & Company

727 Fifth Avenue
New York, NY 10022
tel: 212-755-8000

PORCELAIN

Pozzi Ginori

41 Madison Avenue
New York, NY 10010
tel: 212-213-6884

CANNAREGIO

49

13

26

25

SANTA CROCE

35

27

53

SAN POLO

1

54

28

3   2

12   29

42

11   61

59

19

SAN MARCO

32   41

48

24   15   36   46   16   38

34   10   39

14   18   17

23   45   33   43   51   9

DORSODURO   6   50

4   7   37   8   56

60   44   40

20

55

5
21   22   47

57

30
31

58

GIUDECCA

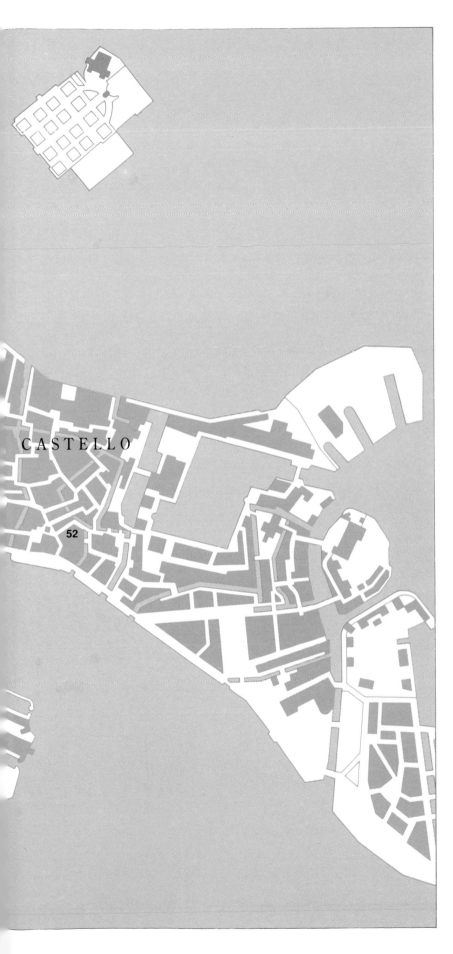

CASTELLO

52

CAMPI

1   San Polo
2   Frari
3   San Rocco
4   San Barnaba
5   San Trovaso
6   Santo Stefano o F. Morosini
7   San Maurizio
8   Santa Maria del Giglio
9   San Moisè
10 Piazza San Marco
11 Santa Maria Formosa
12 San Giovanni e Paolo
13 Ghetto Nuovo
14 Santa Margherita
15 Sant'Angelo

PUBLIC BUILDINGS

16 San Marco
17 Florian
18 La Fenice
19 Palazzo Querini Stampalia
20 Casetta Rossa
21 Squero di San Trovaso
22 Ca' Dario
23 Ca' Rezzonico
24 Palazzo Grassi
25 Ca' d'Oro
26 Palazzo Labia
27 Mercato del Rialto
28 Convento dei Frari
29 San Giovanni e Paolo
30 Casa Tre Occhi
31 Casa Frolo
32 Museo Fortuny

ARTS AND CRAFTS

33 Norélène
34 Mirella Spinella
35 Luigi Bevilacqua
36 Rubelli
37 Trois
38 Jesurum
39 Maria Mazzaron
40 Piazzesi
41 Barutti
42 Laboratorio Artigiano Maschere
43 Pietro Scarpa
44 Zancope
45 R. Pedrina
46 Venini
47 Salviati
48 Pauly
49 Orsini
50 L'Isola
51 Carlo Moretti

RESTAURANTS

52 Corte Sconta
53 Caffè Orientale
54 Alla Madonna
55 Locanda Montin
56 Harry's Bar
57 Harry's Dolci
58 L'Altanella
59 Donna Onesta
60 Furatola
61 Al Mascaron

Further Reading

BLUE GUIDE *Venice*, London 1980/New York 1990

ARSLAN, E. *Gothic Architecture in Venice* (translated A. Engel),
London/ New York 1971

BULL, GEORGE *Venice: The Most Triumplant City*, London 1982/New
York 1981

GRUNDY, MILTON *Venice, an Anthology Guide*, London 1976

HIBBERT, CHRISTOPHER *Venice: The Biography of a City*, London 1988/
New York 1989

HONOUR, HUGH *The Companion Guide to Venice*, London 1965/New
York 1966

JAMES, HENRY *The Aspern Papers*, London 1888 (New York edition
1908)
— *Italian Hours*, Boston 1909
— *The Wings of the Dove*, New York 1902

LANE, F.C. *Venice, a Maritime Republic*, Baltimore 1973
— *Venice and History*, Baltimore 1966

LAURITZEN, PETER L. *Islands and Lagoons of Venice*, New York 1980
— *The Palaces of Venice*, London/New York 1978
— *Venice: A Thousand Years of Culture and Civilisation*,
London/New York 1978
— *Venice Preserved*, London/New York 1986

LEES-MILNE, JAMES *Venetian Evenings*, London 1988

LINKS, J.G. *Venice for Pleasure*, London/New York 1966

LOGAN, OLIVER *Culture and Society in Venice 1470-1790*,
London/New York 1972

LONGWORTH, P. *The Rise and Fall of Venice*, London 1974

LORENZETTI, GUILIO *Venice and its Lagoon* (translated John Guthrie),
Rome 1961

McCARTHY, MARY *Venice Observed*, London/New York 1956

MARTINEAU, JANE and HOPE, JAMES (ed.) *Genius of Venice*,
London/New York 1983

MORRIS, J. *A Venetian Bestiary*, London/New York 1982
— *The Venetian Empire*, London/New York 1980
— *Venice*, London 1960

NORWICH, JOHN JULIUS *A History of Venice*, London/New York 1982
(*Venice, the Rise to Empire*, 1977, and *Venice, the Greatness and the
Fall*, 1981, published as one vol.)

PIGNATTI, T. *Venice* (translated J. Landry), London/New York 1971

PULLAN, B. *A History of Early Renaissance Venice*, London 1973
— *Rich and Poor in Renaissance Venice*, London/Cambridge, MA 1971

ROWDON, MAURICE *The Fall of Venice*, London 1970
— *The Silver Age of Venice*, New York 1970

RUSKIN, JOHN *St Mark's Rest*, London 1877
— *The stones of Venice* (3 vols), London 1851-53

SALVADORI, ANTONIO *101 Buildings To See in Venice*, Venice 1969

SHAW-KENNEDY, R. *Art and Architecture in Venice. The Venice in Peril
Guide*, London 1972 (published in the United States as *Venice
Rediscovered*, Philadelphia 1978)

STEER, JOHN *Venetian Painting: A Concise History*, London 1970/New
York 1979

Index